# DARK MANIPULATION FOR WOMEN

*Alpha Female Tactics for Mastering Power, Control, and Influence through Emotional Intelligence, Femme Fatale Secrets, Dark Feminine Energy, and Magnetic Confidence*

**KARA LAWRENCE**

© **Copyright 2024 - All rights reserved.**

The content contained within this book may not be reproduced, duplicated or transmitted without direct written permission from the author or the publisher.

Under no circumstances will any blame or legal responsibility be held against the publisher, or author, for any damages, reparation, or monetary loss due to the information contained within this book, either directly or indirectly.

**Legal Notice:**

This book is copyright protected. It is only for personal use. You cannot amend, distribute, sell, use, quote or paraphrase any part, or the content within this book, without the consent of the author or publisher.

**Disclaimer Notice:**

Please note the information contained within this document is for educational and entertainment purposes only. All effort has been executed to present accurate, up to date, reliable, complete information. No warranties of any kind are declared or implied. Readers acknowledge that the author is not engaged in the rendering of legal, financial, medical or professional advice. The content within this book has been derived from various sources. Please consult a licensed professional before attempting any techniques outlined in this book.

By reading this document, the reader agrees that under no circumstances is the author responsible for any losses, direct or indirect, that are incurred as a result of the use of the information contained within this document, including, but not limited to, errors, omissions, or inaccuracies.

# Table of Contents

Introduction .................................................................................... 1

**Chapter 1** ...................................................................................... 4

**Embracing Your Inner Alpha Female** ........................................ 4

  Key Characteristics and Mindset ............................................... 5

    Courage and Confidence ........................................................ 5

    Resilience and Determination ................................................ 5

    Empathy and Compassion ..................................................... 5

    Strategic Thinking and Leadership ....................................... 6

  Building Self-Confidence and Assertiveness ............................ 6

    What is Self-Awareness ......................................................... 6

    Self-Acceptance ..................................................................... 7

    Affirmations and Positive Self-Talk ..................................... 7

    Reinforce Positive Thoughts ................................................. 7

    Setting Boundaries ................................................................ 7

    Body Language ...................................................................... 8

  Overcoming Societal Stereotypes and Expectations ................ 8

    Reframe Negative Beliefs ..................................................... 9

    Build a Support Network ...................................................... 9

    Celebrate Diversity .............................................................. 10

    Find Role Models ................................................................ 10

  Real-Life Examples of Alpha Females ..................................... 11

    Marie Curie ........................................................................... 11

    Harriet Tubman .................................................................... 11

    Sheryl Sandberg ................................................................... 12

    Malala Yousafzai .................................................................. 12

    Everyday Alpha Females ................................................................ 12

    Segue .............................................................................................. 13

**Chapter 2** ............................................................................................ 14

**The Psychology of Dark Manipulation** ........................................... 14

    Understanding Human Behavior and Motivation ......................... 14

    Maslow's Hierarchy of Needs ........................................................ 15

    Recognizing Emotional Triggers and Leverage Points................. 17

        Identifying Triggers ................................................................... 17

        Building Connection ................................................................. 17

        Practical Application................................................................. 18

        Assessment of Response ........................................................... 18

        The Role of Emotions ............................................................... 19

    Ethical Boundaries in Manipulation ............................................. 19

        Reflective Practices................................................................... 20

    Case Studies on Successful Manipulative Tactics ....................... 20

        Corporate Stories....................................................................... 21

        Personal Relationships .............................................................. 21

        Friendships ................................................................................ 21

        Cultural Perspectives................................................................. 22

    Segue .............................................................................................. 22

**Chapter 3** ............................................................................................ 24

**Communication Strategies for Influence** ........................................ 24

    Mastering Verbal and Non-Verbal Communication Skills.......... 24

        Developing Verbal and Non-verbal Skills for Effective Influence
................................................................................................... 25

        Vocal Aspects ............................................................................ 25

  Mirroring ........................................................................ 26

 Using Persuasive Language and Arguments .............................. 26

  Use the Problem-Solution-Benefit Framework ...................... 26

  Use Rhetorical Techniques ................................................... 27

  Call to Action ..................................................................... 27

  Monitor Engagement .......................................................... 28

 Active Listening and Observing Micro-Expressions ................. 28

  Reflective Listening ............................................................ 28

  Micro-Expressions .............................................................. 29

  Comforting Environments ................................................... 29

 Tailoring Your Message to Different Audiences ....................... 30

  Simplifying Ideas ............................................................... 31

  Share Stories ...................................................................... 31

 Segue ....................................................................................... 32

**Chapter 4 ..................................................................................... 34**

**Building Emotional Intelligence .................................................. 34**

 Understanding and Managing Your Emotions ........................... 35

  Journaling .......................................................................... 35

  Mindfulness Practices ......................................................... 35

  Ask for Feedback ............................................................... 36

 Empathy: The Key to Understanding Others ............................. 37

  Define Empathy ................................................................. 37

  Practicing Empathy ............................................................ 37

  Recognizing Non-Verbal Cues ............................................ 37

  Showing Compassion ......................................................... 38

 Reading and Responding to Emotional Cues ............................. 38

    Respond Appropriately .................................................................. 38

    Emotional Responsiveness ............................................................ 39

    Create a Feedback Loop ............................................................... 40

Techniques for Emotional Regulation and Resilience ................. 41

    Breathing Exercises ....................................................................... 41

    Reframing Your Thoughts ............................................................ 41

    Building Resilience ....................................................................... 42

    Self-Care ........................................................................................ 42

Segue ................................................................................................... 43

## Chapter 5 ........................................................................................... 44

## Assertive Leadership in Personal Relationships ......................... 44

Setting Boundaries and Sticking to Them ........................................ 44

    Creating Your Boundaries ............................................................ 45

    Communicating Your Boundaries ............................................... 45

    Maintaining Your Boundaries ...................................................... 46

    Recognize the Signs ..................................................................... 46

Balancing Assertiveness With Compassion ..................................... 47

    Understanding Assertiveness vs. Aggression ............................. 47

    Using Compassion in Conflict ..................................................... 48

    Assessing the Right Moments ..................................................... 48

Transformative Conversations With Partners ................................ 49

    Ask Yourself Questions ................................................................ 49

    Creating Safe Dialogue ................................................................ 50

    Use Your Body Language ............................................................ 50

    Follow-up and Accountability ...................................................... 50

Strategies for Handling Conflict Effectively ..................................... 51

Effective Communication .......................................................... 51

Compromising ......................................................................... 51

Segue ............................................................................................ 52

## Chapter 6 ................................................................................... 53
## Leveraging Femininity as Power ................................................ 53

Breaking Down Misconceptions About Femininity .................... 53

Empathy and Nurturing ........................................................ 54

Vulnerability .......................................................................... 54

Embracing Your Unique Characteristics ............................... 54

Celebrating Approaches ........................................................ 55

Understanding These Elements ............................................. 55

Provide Support ..................................................................... 55

Combining Grace With Strength .................................................. 56

Grace in Communication ...................................................... 56

Integrating Strength and Grace ............................................. 57

Meditation ............................................................................. 57

Learn From Others ................................................................ 57

Practical Examples ................................................................ 57

Find Specific Activities ......................................................... 58

Using Charm as a Strategic Tool ................................................. 58

Elements of Charm ................................................................ 58

Incorporation Tips ................................................................. 59

Defusing Tension .................................................................. 60

Real-Life Examples ............................................................... 60

Maintaining Authenticity While Asserting Power ...................... 61

Self-Awareness ...................................................................... 61

    Strategies to Express Yourself ................................................... 61

    Building Relationships ................................................................ 62

  Segue .................................................................................................. 63

## Chapter 7 .................................................................................... 64

## Developing a Strategist's Mindset ........................................... 64

  Identifying Your Goals and Desired Outcomes ........................... 65

    Understanding Your Core Values ............................................... 65

    Defining Specific Goals ............................................................... 65

    Visualizing Desired Outcomes .................................................... 66

    Outlining Purposeful Strategies .................................................. 66

  Crafting a Step-by-Step Strategic Plan ......................................... 68

    Setting Timelines ........................................................................ 68

    Clarify Resources ........................................................................ 69

    Evaluating Obstacles .................................................................. 69

    Think Ahead ............................................................................... 69

  Adapting to Changing Circumstances and Feedback ................... 70

    Feedback .................................................................................... 71

    Adjusting Your Strategies ........................................................... 71

    Continuous Learning .................................................................. 71

  Examples of Effective Dark Manipulation ................................... 72

    Personal Relationships ............................................................... 72

    Professional Settings .................................................................. 72

    Examining Social Manipulations ................................................ 73

    Investigating Modern Media ...................................................... 73

  Segue .................................................................................................. 74

## Chapter 8 .................................................................................... 75

**Healthier Dynamics in Professional Relationships** ............... 75

   Establishing Your Presence and Authority at Work .............. 76

      Identify Your Core Values and Skills ................................. 76

      Mastering Body Language ................................................ 77

      Verbal Language ............................................................... 77

      Leveraging Feedback ....................................................... 78

   Negotiation Tactics to Achieve Desired Results .................... 78

      Preparation and Research ................................................. 78

      Using Assertive Language ................................................ 79

      Finding Win-Win Scenarios ............................................. 79

      Handling Objections Gracefully ....................................... 80

   Building Alliances and Networks Strategically ..................... 80

      Identify Key Stakeholders ................................................ 81

      Networking Events ........................................................... 81

      Follow-Up and Maintain .................................................. 82

   Handling Competition and Politics Effectively ..................... 82

      Understanding Workplace Dynamics ............................... 83

      Engaging in Competition ................................................. 83

      Building Rapport ............................................................. 84

   Segue ..................................................................................... 84

**Chapter 9** ................................................................................. 86

**Transforming Into a Femme Fatale** ........................................ 86

   Traits of a Femme Fatale: Confidence, Mystery, and Charm ..... 86

      Confidence ........................................................................ 87

      Mystery ............................................................................. 87

      Charm ............................................................................... 88

Incorporating Intrigue Into Your Persona ..........................................89
    Personal Stories ..........................................89
    Selective Sharing ..........................................89
    Non-Verbal Communication ..........................................90
    Engaging Conversations ..........................................90
    Balance Openness ..........................................90

Using Allure to Captivate and Influence ..........................................91
    Understanding Allure ..........................................91
    Awareness of Surroundings ..........................................92
    Empowering Others ..........................................92
    Tactful Influence ..........................................93

Maintaining Control and Desirability ..........................................94
    Boundaries ..........................................94
    Self-Care ..........................................94
    Self-Improvement ..........................................95
    Decision-Making ..........................................96

Segue ..........................................97

## Chapter 10 ..........................................98

## Sustaining Long-Term Success and Influence ..........................................98

Continually Refining Your Skills and Strategies ..........................................99
    Educational Resources ..........................................99
    Self-Reflection ..........................................99
    Journaling ..........................................100
    Seeking Feedback ..........................................100
    Growth Mindset ..........................................100

Balancing Power Dynamics Sustainably ..........................................101

- Be Clear About Your Boundaries ............................................ 101
- Avoid Overreliance .................................................................. 102
- Recognizing Distortion ........................................................... 102
- Adapting to Evolving Personal and Professional Landscapes .. 103
  - Building a Flexible Strategic Plan.......................................... 104
  - Embrace Technology............................................................. 105
- Lessons From Long-Term Success Stories ................................ 105
  - Lisa ......................................................................................... 106
  - Maria ...................................................................................... 106
- Segue .......................................................................................... 108

**Conclusion** ................................................................................ 109

**References** ................................................................................ 113

# INTRODUCTION

Navigating the world as a woman can be tough, but luckily, there is a solution to the vast majority of issues you might be facing. Whether you are a young professional climbing the corporate ladder, a woman facing challenges in her own personal life, or a feminist exploring gender dynamics, this book is absolutely perfect for you. This is not your run-of-the-mill self-help book; it's a manual to help you unleash your inner Alpha female.

So, you might be wondering what exactly makes this book different from others.

Well, the main objective of this book is pretty straightforward: to help empower you. I will be helping you dive deeper into the art of dark manipulation strategies, but before you get the wrong idea, let's clarify that this isn't about deceiving anyone. It's about mastering various strategies to help you regain control of your own life, allowing you to shape your own narrative with confidence and assertiveness. It's much like playing a game of chess while people around you might be playing checkers. You hold all the pieces in your own hands, and you can make the best move to ensure that you are winning in life.

If you ever find yourself overshadowed in your relationships, or like you always need to compromise or play second best, just know that you are not alone. There are many women who are also struggling to balance their own desires with the expectations that society puts on us. Society expects us to be police and accommodating, and we need to avoid making waves. But deep down, there will always be a small part of you who craves more, a part that wants to be the leader and not the follower. Someone who wants to be unapologetically strong and self-confident. This book will act as your toolkit to unlock all your hidden strengths in the daily struggles we face.

Imagine this: You are able to walk into any room with your head held high and an aura that shows unshakable confidence. People will start noticing and respecting you without you having to say a single word. This will help you become seen, heard, valued, and admired. Knowing your worth and using it to your advantage is the most important part of becoming an alpha female. You will no longer feel like a supporting character in your own story; instead, you will be the leading lady, pushing your life in the direction you want it to go.

Now you might be asking, B*ut how do we reach this*?

Throughout this manuscript, you will become equipped with various powerful tools and insights. You will learn how to use the subtle art of manipulation to position yourself as a force to be reckoned with. These include communication techniques in both your personal and professional life. Plus, we will delve into how you can develop a strategic mindset so you can anticipate and navigate the various challenges you might face with finesse.

This book will act as your own personal playbook, with each chapter strategically designed to give you the practical skills you need and help you implement them immediately. This includes everything from reading people's intentions to influencing outcomes. You will get an edge that will set you apart from the crowd. This journey might not be easy when you start out, and you might need to start changing your mindset so you can rethink some of your ingrained beliefs. But the end results are well worth the effort.

Throughout this book, you will also find real-life scenarios and case studies, showing you some concrete examples of how you should be using these strategies. Whether you're dealing with a difficult boss, you are involved in a difficult relationship, or you just want to start asserting yourself more confidently, you will find all the insights you need in the pages of this book. By the end, you will have a toolkit full of techniques to make yourself absolutely unstoppable.

Let's not forget the power of a community. The journey towards becoming an alpha female might feel lonely at times, but keep in mind that there are various women who have gone through the same thing. They have faced the same struggles and came out stronger, wiser, and more empowered. Reading this book means that you will be joining a tribe of incredible women who refuse to settle for mediocrity.

Now, I would like to mention that you will not be changing who you are by the end of this book; instead, you will be embracing your authentic self and amplifying it. It's about recognizing the power you already have and learning how to use it effectively. So buckle up and get ready for this transformative ride. There is no better time than now to redefine your relationships and reshape your life. The world needs more alpha females, and you are one of them.

Remember that keeping an open mind and a willing heart is essential. You need to be willing to challenge yourself, step out of your comfort zone, and grow in ways you never thought possible. It's your time to shine, to take control, and to become the best version of yourself.

Welcome to this exciting journey, and let's dive right in so you can start unleashing your inner alpha female and start changing the game.

## Chapter 1
# EMBRACING YOUR INNER ALPHA FEMALE

Allowing your inner alpha female to surface means reshaping your mindset to combine strength, confidence, and empathy. It's not just about being the loudest and most assertive person; it's about embracing and understanding the qualities that make you stand out.

This includes handling curveballs with resilience so you can start forging meaning relationships with dark manipulation strategies. This chapter will help guide you to harness these traits and navigate the different realms of your life effectively. This chapter will help you see what sets you apart as an alpha female, including characteristics like courage, confidence, resilience, and strategic thinking. You will also learn about taking calculated risks and techniques for building self-confidence, setting boundaries, and adopting a mindset that sees challenges as opportunities for growth. By the end of this chapter, you will have a comprehensive understanding of how to embrace your inner Alpha female and assert yourself.

## Key Characteristics and Mindset

Understanding and embodying certain traits is the first step to creating a stronger and more confident mindset. So, let's take a look at what you need to start standing out.

### *Courage and Confidence*

Courage and confidence are the first traits. Your journey starts with your willingness to take risks and make the right moves when adversity strikes. This means that you need to step out of your comfort zone and embrace the unknown. Whether it's speaking up during a meeting or pursuing a new career opportunity, you should never let fear hold you back. Instead, confront challenges head-on with the knowledge that each step will help you grow. Confidence comes from accepting yourself and acknowledging your own self-worth. It's about saying, "I'm capable," and proving it through your actions. Confidence, however, doesn't mean you should be arrogant; it's the self-assurance that others can sense and respect.

### *Resilience and Determination*

Resilience and determination are the second two sets of traits. These help you with life's curveballs. As an alpha female, you need to understand that failure is not a reflection of your abilities, but rather an opportunity to learn and improve. Adopting this mindset will allow you to persevere even in tough times. For example, if you encounter a setback at work, you should analyze what went wrong, learn from it, and come back stronger. Your tenacity is rooted in your belief that nothing is impossible, and every challenge you face is another hurdle you need to overcome in order to reach success.

### *Empathy and Compassion*

Empathy and compassion are the third set of traits, which might get overlooked, but they are still essential qualities of an alpha female. While it's important to have strength and confidence, you need to understand and connect with others to become a great leader. Empathy allows you to see situations from another person's perspective while building mutual respect and trust. Compassion lets you lead while being kind and considerate, which makes those around you feel valued and understood. For example, in a team setting, you might prioritize listening to your colleagues' concerns and provide them with the support they need. This balance between strength and empathy creates a harmonious and productive environment for anyone trying to reshape their mindset.

## *Strategic Thinking and Leadership*

Finally, there is strategic thinking and leadership. These traits help set you apart from the others in your professional and personal circle. These traits also help you foresee future challenges and opportunities, which enables you to make informed and effective decisions. Strategic thinking allows you to analyze data, consider long-term outcomes, and plan the necessary steps. With the leadership trait, you can guide your team with clarity and vision. You can use insights to navigate complex situations, ensuring your goals are efficiently met. As an alpha female, you can also inspire those around you to think and act proactively and create a culture where they appreciate innovation and resilience.

Now that you know about these traits, you can start cultivating them before becoming an alpha female. Let's move on to discussing how you can build your self-confidence and use your assertiveness.

## **Building Self-Confidence and Assertiveness**

Building your self-confidence and assertiveness is important to embody these traits. Keep in mind that building confidence is not something that happens overnight; it starts with a deep sense of self-awareness and self-acceptance. These elements are crucial in creating a strong, empowered presence in your life.

## *What is Self-Awareness*

Self-awareness is knowing who you are, including your strengths, weaknesses, values, and aspirations in life. You need to reflect on these aspects to get clarity and direction in your life. For example, you might consider buying a journal to record your thoughts, achievements, and areas you want to improve. This direct self-reflection allows you to understand the driving force behind you and what you need to do to become an alpha female.

## *Self-Acceptance*

Self-acceptance and self-awareness go hand-in-hand. Self-acceptance is about accepting and embracing every aspect of yourself, even those you might not like. Nobody's perfect and learning how to accept your weaknesses will help you build a solid foundation for confidence. Buy a gratitude journal and start acknowledging your successes and the qualities that make you unique. This will help you shift your perspective and create a more positive self-image.

## *Affirmations and Positive Self-Talk*

These two powerful tools can be used to help you combat negative thoughts from entering your mind. Replacing self-criticism with constructive and optimistic language will help you reshape your mindset. Start your day with affirmations like, "I'm capable," "I deserve success," or "I'm confident." These simple statements can gradually and effectively help you transform the internal dialogue you use, which leads to stronger self-esteem.

## *Reinforce Positive Thoughts*

As an alpha female, you need to remind yourself of the positive aspects that show how competent and resilient you are daily. This helps break down any self-doubt you have so you can build a stronger, more nurturing inner voice.

## *Setting Boundaries*

The ability to set boundaries is possibly one of the most important steps to building your assertiveness. You might struggle with this because you are afraid that you are disappointing others or being rude. However, when you learn to set personal boundaries, you are maintaining the respect you get from others while taking care of your own well-being. Practice saying *no* in low-stake situations if you want to build your confidence. Remember, you need to prioritize your own needs and expectations above those of others.

For example, if a colleague wants you to take on extra work, you have the right to say no. You can say something like, "I appreciate you thinking of me, but I already have too much work at the moment." These boundaries will foster respect, which leads to healthier relationships built on mutual respect.

## *Body Language*

The body language you use is another important aspect of showing your confidence. Non-verbal cues can often be louder than words. Additionally, when you adopt an assertive posture, you impact the way others view you. Stand tall with your shoulders back and your head high in every situation. Maintaining eye contact during conversations will also show engagement and self-assurance.

Other signals of confidence include a firm handshake, a steady gaze, and deliberate movements. Pay attention to your tone of voice and avoid filters like "um" or "uh" during conversations. These small changes in your non-verbal communication style can enhance your overall presence and effectiveness when interacting with others.

Remember, in order to grow your confidence and assertiveness, it is an ongoing process. Commit to ongoing self-improvement by setting specific yet achievable goals for yourself. Don't forget to evaluate your progress and celebrate your milestones, no matter how small. Over time, you will start solidifying your transformation.

## **Overcoming Societal Stereotypes and Expectations**

Embracing your inner alpha female requires stepping away from the constraints that society has, which allow you to thrive as your true self. To start, look at the societal pressures you face in your life. These pressures can dictate the way you behave, dress, and speak. From a young age, girls are bombarded with messages about what's appropriate or "feminine." When you understand these expectations, you will get a clearer view of why certain choices may seem uncomfortable or forced.

Imagine growing up hearing that being loud or assertive is unladylike. This can diminish your confidence, making it more challenging to speak up in a professional setting. Being aware of these pressures allows you to question their validity. Determine whether these expectations are a true reflection of who you are, or are they the remnants of outdated norms?

### *Reframe Negative Beliefs*

Reframing your negative beliefs is the first step to overcoming societal expectations. Negativity gets thrown at us when we don't conform to standards. However, these criticisms can fuel your empowerment. Think about it: being labeled "bossy" may be negative, but when you take it as a sign of your leadership qualities, then it translates to increased self-confidence instead of self-doubt.

To do this, you need to take every negative remark and turn it into a positive affirmation. If someone says you are aggressive, then remind yourself that you are assertive and decisive. This perspective shift won't be immediate, but with regular practice, it can help you build resilience against negativity. Create a habit of transforming the judgement from society into personal strengths so you can feel more empowered.

### *Build a Support Network*

Having a support network backing you up is another important aspect of building self-confidence and overcoming society's expectations. Surround yourself with like-minded people who will support you on your journey. A strong network can also give you emotional support, advice, and collaborate with you on projects. It's important to find communities, whether they are professional networks, social groups, or online forums, where mutual respect and encouragement is normal.

Networking events that specifically cater to women in your industry or social circles are a great place to start building your support network. These events give you a platform to share your experiences with other women with similar struggles. This can make you feel validated and motivated to continue on your journey. These connections can also open doors to opportunities you might not have found on your own. Collaborating with a support network helps to amplify your voice, making it more difficult for limiting stereotypes to silence you.

### Celebrate Diversity

Don't forget to celebrate your diversity in femininity. Remember, there is no user manual to being feminine. Our society promotes a narrow view of what womanhood should be, but true feminine power comes from embracing our individuality and differences. Whether you are softspoken or outspoken, nurturing or competitive, your vision of femininity is valid.

### Find Role Models

There are many role models who are overcoming the expectations of society. These prominent females include Serena Williams, who shows her strength both on and off the tennis court, or Malala Yousafzai, who fights for education far beyond traditional gender roles, showing the diversity of feminine power.

By understanding and valuing our diverse expressions of femininity, we can break down the notion that there is only one correct way to be a woman. This acceptance extends to every facet of life, including personal, professional, and societal. It helps create an environment where differences are not only tolerated but celebrated. By doing this, we pave the way for future generations to express themselves freely, without fear of judgment or ridicule.

Challenging societal norms and stereotypes involves various things, including:

- Identify the pressures shaping your decisions and recognize their impact.
- Reframe negative beliefs into empowering affirmations.

- Build a support network to strengthen your resolve and amplify your voice.
- Celebrate the diversity in your femininity; understand everyone's journey is uniquely powerful.

**Real-Life Examples of Alpha Females**

This section will give you some real-life examples of powerful alpha females who made their mark in history, in modern times, and even in the lives of their communities. We will discuss how these women used their unique traits and strategies discussed in this chapter to overcome obstacles and achieve greatness. These women faced various challenges, but they didn't let them stand in their way.

*Marie Curie*

One inspiring woman is Marie Curie, the first woman to win a Nobel Prize and the first one to win a Nobel Prize in two different scientific fields—Physics and Chemistry—which were primarily male-dominated fields. Curie's groundbreaking work in radioactivity was done when women were rarely seen in science. Despite facing gender bias and doing her research in poorly equipped labs, she persevered. Her resilience and resolve increased scientific knowledge while paving the way for women who wanted to be scientists in the future (The Nobel Prize, 2024).

*Harriet Tubman*

The second amazing women is Harriet Tubman, an African American abolitionist who escaped slavery and returned years later to lead hundreds of people who faced the same challenges to freedom through the Underground Railroad. Tubman's courage and unwavering sense of justice helped her challenge and dismantle a deeply entrenched system of oppression. Imagine the strength it had to have taken for her to risk her life for the freedom of others. Her story reminds us that true leaders often involve making sacrifices for the greater good (Dawson, n.d.).

### Sheryl Sandberg

You might already know about Sheryl Sandberg, who is the COO of Facebook and the author of "Lean In." Sandberg's career has been marked by her advocacy for women's empowerment in the workplace. She shares valuable insights on navigating the corporate ladder while pushing for more inclusive workplaces where equity is valued. Her transparency about the struggles she faced and the strategies she used makes her journey relatable and instructive to so many women who are aiming to break the glass ceiling (Wikipedia Contributors, n.d.-a).

### Malala Yousafzai

This amazing women, Malala Yousafzai, is a Pakistani activist for female education and one of the youngest Nobel Prize laureates. Her bravery in advocating for girls' education in the face of adversity is inspiring. She was shot by the Taliban for her activism and survived; she also continued her mission with an even more unbreakable drive. Her story demonstrates how standing up for what you believe in can be powerful, no matter the cost (Wikipedia Contributors, n.d.-b).

### Everyday Alpha Females

Don't just get caught up with all the famous women. There are women in our everyday lives who walk next to us. Consider a single mom who juggles multiple jobs to provide for her children while still finding time to volunteer at their school. Or the young professional who advocates for equal pay for everyone, opening up difficult but necessary conversations with management. These ordinary women have alpha traits with their determination, resilience, and willingness to confront challenges head-on. Their stories spark conversations about empowerment and remind us that you don't need a high-profile position to make a significant impact.

Consider the community leaders who became alpha females. These women might not seek the spotlight, but their efforts create lasting positive changes within their communities. For example, the local activist who tirelessly works to improve neighborhood safety, address homelessness, or advocate for better educational opportunities. Their alpha characteristics are evident in their ability to mobilize resources, inspire others, and bring tangible improvements in their communities.

These stories show us the traits of alpha females: resilience, courage, determination, and strategic thinking; and they are not confined to one domain. Whether through historical contexts, modern-day scenarios, everyday settings, or community engagement, these traits empower women to break barriers and effect change. By embodying these qualities, you can assert yourself in your personal and professional life, leaving a lasting impact on the world around you.

**Segue**

I hope you enjoyed discussing the defining traits of an alpha female and how they can empower you in your personal and professional life. From embracing courage and confidence to showing your resilience and determination. We also discussed the strength and empathy you need as an alpha female. These qualities help you navigate challenges and enable you to build meaningful connections. By embracing these traits, you can pave the way for an assertive and confident presence. Remember that growth is an ongoing journey. Keep practicing self-awareness and self-acceptance, use positive affirmations, and set clear boundaries. Incorporating these practices into your daily life will enhance your confidence and assertiveness and inspire those around you to do the same.

## Chapter 2
# THE PSYCHOLOGY OF DARK MANIPULATION

This chapter will shed some light on the psychology of manipulation and the dark tactics people use to influence others. Dark manipulation doesn't only involve tactics; it also includes understanding human behavior, emotions, and needs. Breaking down these psychological strategies will give you a deeper understanding of how others might manipulate you and how you can use these strategies to manipulate others. This chapter will delve into the nuanced work of dark psychological manipulation. This includes emotional triggers and psychological points manipulators exploit, so you can recognize and effectively respond to them. You will see how understanding basic human needs and motivations can enhance your ability to connect with others and achieve your goals. By the end of this chapter, you will have a deeper understanding of the dynamics at play and you will have the strategies needed to confidently handle manipulative strategies.

## Understanding Human Behavior and Motivation

This section will help you understand human behavior and what motivates others to do certain things. One of the main strategies we will look into is Maslow's Hierarchy of Needs and how you can use this pyramid to find the best way of handling certain situations and people (McLeod, n.d.).

## Maslow's Hierarchy of Needs

To navigate your relationships effectively, it's important to understand the reasons behind human actions and desires. One tool we will discuss is Maslow's Hierarchy of Needs, created by Abraham Maslow. His framework explains the fundamental needs that drive behavior in humans and how understanding these needs can help you identify the motivation of others, which is a powerful tool for influence (McLeod, n.d.).

## Understanding the Pyramid

Maslow's Hierarchy of Needs is shown as a pyramid with five levels. At the bottom is basic needs like food, water, and shelter (psychological needs). These things are needed for surviving everyday life. Once this need is satisfied, people will move up to the next level, which is the safety need. This involves physical, financial, and health safety.

The third level is the social needs of humans, including love, friendship, and belonging. As humans, we are social creatures seeking connections and relationships. Moving one up, we find the esteem needs of humans, which involves respect, self-esteem, and recognition from others. The point of the pyramid is where we will find self-actualization needs. The self-actualization needs of humans include the pursuit of personal growth, fulfilling your own potential, and achieving your personal goals.

Understanding this hierarchy helps you categorize people under each level of the pyramid so you can tailor your approach on how to connect with them. For example, if someone is struggling with financial insecurity (a safety need), then they won't need emotional support or a deeper connection. This is because their financial needs need to be addressed first. Understanding these layers lets you meet people where they are, which helps you build more meaningful and cooperative relationships.

## How to Use Maslow's Hierarchy

This awareness can create a framework so you can see how they react within certain situations. For example, if you know someone values self-esteem needs, then you can offer them genuine praise and recognition to motivate them to cooperate or take the desired actions. On the other hand, if their social needs are unmet, then you can create opportunities for them to be included and feel valued. This will help you strengthen your relationships with them and make them more receptive to your influence and, ultimately, your manipulation.

Imagine dealing with a stressed and distant colleague who is not performing in their job. By taking a look at their behavior and listening to what they have to say, you might find their need for job security (safety need) is not being met. You can reassure them or help them find stability to create more effective collaboration.

By understanding the unmet needs of those around you, you can make your interactions more strategic. Using the art of dark manipulation is about influencing those around you while appearing empathetic. This helps you align your goals with the needs of others, ensuring mutual benefit.

For example, if you enter a negotiation understanding the other party has a need for self-actualization, then frame your offer to align with their personal growth and aspirations. Having this awareness in everyday situations can help you in different ways. Let's say you're a manager trying to improve your team dynamics. Understanding the needs of your team will create an environment where you can use dark manipulation to make everyone feel secured, valued, and motivated.

Understanding the needs of your personal relationships can also help you build more meaningful connections. For example, if your partner has high self-esteem needs, then you need to acknowledge their achievements more and give them sincere compliments. Contrarily, if they have more basic needs, then you need to give them more practical support to get the best cooperation from them.

Using this framework in everyday life can help you exert influence over people and by aligning these strategies with what genuinely matters to you and them, ensures that your actions are perceived as supportive instead of manipulative. This helps you create an environment where trust, cooperation, and mutual respect thrive, creating a win-win situation for everyone (with you being the ultimate winner).

## Recognizing Emotional Triggers and Leverage Points

Emotional triggers and leverage points play an important role in how you shape your interactions and outcomes, especially in personal relationships. Understanding these components impacts how you navigate your personal and professional life.

### *Identifying Triggers*

Emotional triggers cause a strong emotional response. Recognizing the most common emotional triggers in your interpersonal interactions is the first step towards leveraging them for a positive outcome. Some of the most common emotional triggers include the feeling of inadequacy, fear of rejection, and the desire for validation.

For example, when someone feels like they are unheard or dismissed, it can trigger feelings of inadequacy. Their reaction can then be anger, sadness, or defensiveness. By identifying these triggers, you can tailor your approach to avoid provoking these negative emotions.

Start by observing the reactions of others to various topics and situations. Are they sensitive about their work performance? Do they react strongly to criticism? These observations can give you valuable insights into what drives their emotional responses.

### *Building Connection*

There are various strategies you can use to help build connections in your personal and professional lives. Some of the most common ones include active listening and mirroring.

Active listening is being fully present and concentrating on what the other person is saying without interrupting. This shows that you are listening and gives you the ability to understand their perspective.

Mirroring involves mimicking the other person's body language, tone, and expressions, which creates a sense of familiarity and trust, making the other person more comfortable and open to your influence.

## *Practical Application*

After identifying emotional triggers and building a connection, it's time to put some valuable strategies in place. For example, adjusting your requests or suggestions to align with the emotional needs and desires of others.

For example, if you're negotiating a raise with your boss, you can frame your request to highlight your contributions and how it impacts the team and company. Show your commitment and enthusiasm for future projects, connecting your achievements with the company's goals. This will eliminate any insecurities and show you are an asset to the company.

You can use emotional understanding in your personal relationships to address issues in a way that validates the other person's feelings. You can use timing to your advantage by choosing the right time to bring up sensitive topics. This makes a significant difference in the outcome. You need to find a time when everyone is relaxed and receptive if you want the best outcome.

## *Assessment of Response*

Establishing how different people react to emotional stimuli is important if you want to create an approach where your interactions are successful. Look at their verbal and non-verbal communication. Establish if they are maintaining eye contact, smiling, or showing signs of engagement, or are they distant, fidgety, or defensive?

The other person's tone and word choice can give you valuable insights. Positive responses include enthusiastic agreement or thoughtful questions. Negative reactions might include short, curt replies or when the other person avoids eye contact.

Depending on these insights, you can adapt your approach accordingly. If you notice signs of discomfort or disengagement, then you need to take a step back and reassess the situation. You might find that your message didn't resonate or your timing for the conversation was off. This means that you might need to take a measured response, like acknowledging the other person's feelings, take a break, and then return to the conversation.

## *The Role of Emotions*

Emotions play a significant role in decision-making, and understanding their role is crucial if you want to master dark manipulation. Decisions are often made based on the emotions people feel in the moment instead of using logical reasoning.

Understanding and finding emotional vulnerabilities will also give you an advantage in planning your conversations. For example, if you know someone craves approval, then appeal to that desire when pitching your request. When using dark manipulation, this means exploiting their vulnerabilities to align with your communications with their emotional landscape to get your desired outcome.

By regulating your emotions, you can maintain your composure and authority during stressful situations. Emotional regulation techniques like deep breathing, mindfulness, and positive visualization can help you manage stress and keep you grounded in difficult situations. It can also help with your dark manipulation strategies.

## **Ethical Boundaries in Manipulation**

When incorporating dark manipulation into your daily life and negotiations, consider the ethical boundaries so you don't come across as manipulative. Continue to respect the autonomy of others and their dignity. This includes an understanding of the ethics within this context. Ethics with manipulation can be a complex subject, but it revolves around the principles of right and wrong that guide individual behaviors.

When it comes to manipulation, it's more important because manipulation means that you are influencing others to do what you need them to do. Therefore, it's important to approach even dark manipulation with a moral compass.

Recognize the boundaries linked to influence with your dark manipulation strategies. Ethical manipulation respects the individuality and freedom of others, not to control but to encourage certain behaviors. For example, if you're helping someone make a choice that benefits them without deceiving them, that's ethical. It might seem unethical to trick people into a decision for your gain, but that is what dark manipulation is all about. Therefore, you need to establish what you find ethical when using dark manipulation so you can create a framework where actions are examined and evaluated against personal moral standards.

There are two different types of manipulation: empowerment and exploitative. *Empowering* manipulation means that you are uplifting others by motivating them to pursue their own dreams by highlighting their strengths. The manipulative type encourages personal growth and self-worth. On the other hand, *exploitative* or dark manipulation involves using the other person's vulnerabilities to your advantage. For example, getting someone to do something they won't normally do.

## *Reflective Practices*

It's extremely important to incorporate reflective practices into your manipulation strategy. Self-reflection allows you to evaluate your intentions and the potential impact of your actions. Reflective practices also involve assessing past actions to determine whether they were ethical or crossed into exploitation. This ongoing evaluation ensures that you continue to use manipulation as a tool for positive outcomes.

## **Case Studies on Successful Manipulative Tactics**

This section offers some real-life examples with valuable insights into dark manipulation. By taking a look at these corporate success stories, personal relationships, and cultural perspectives, you can get a clearer picture of how manipulation works.

## Corporate Stories

Let's start with corporate success stories. In a high-stakes business environment, manipulation can often manifest itself in subtle but powerful ways. This case study is about a mid-level manager aiming to get a promotion at the company she was working for. She employed tactics like strategically withholding information and being selectively transparent in other instances to create a favorable impression with managers and individuals who are higher up in the company, all while undermining her competitors. This savvy executive used her charm and strategic alliances to rise through the ranks quickly. By selectively sharing credit with key players and subtly planting doubts about her rivals, she climbed the corporate ladder. Remember, these tactics might seem ruthless, but they are effective and acceptable in a competitive setting.

## Personal Relationships

The following case study revolves around personal relationships and how manipulation can take on a more intimate and emotional form. Think of one partner using guilt-tripping and passive-aggression to control the other person. For example, reminding their partner about past mistakes to try to extract feelings of guilt and compliance. Another example is emotional blackmail, where one person threatens to end the relationship or withdraw affection. Another strategic dark manipulation tactic is using your sexuality to get what you want from your partner.

## Friendships

When it comes to friendships, use subtle techniques like playing the victim to gain sympathy or use flattery to achieve your desired outcome. Imagine a scenario where a friend is constantly expecting you to do favors but rarely does the same for you. They might manipulate you by praising you just before asking for another favor, making it difficult for you to refuse without feeling guilty. These tactics exploit emotional vulnerabilities and can significantly affect the nature of personal relationships.

## Cultural Perspectives

Considering cultural perspectives, manipulation can vary widely across different societies. In some cultures, manipulation may be overtly practiced and even socially accepted, while in others, it might be more covert and frowned upon. For example, in certain collectivist cultures, indirect communication and saving face are crucial. Here, manipulation involves using intermediaries to convey messages or employing non-verbal cues to influence others' perceptions without direct confrontation. Contrastingly, in individualistic cultures, where directness is often valued, manipulation might take the form of persuasive rhetoric and assertive negotiation tactics.

It's important to recognize the patterns of manipulation and be vigilant against them. You should also be emotionally aware when using dark manipulation tactics in your life. Using manipulation tactics effectively requires you to understand your own emotions and those of the people you are trying to manipulate.

Taking these insights into account will help you, as a young woman and professional, better equip yourself to use manipulation proactively throughout various scenarios. Recognizing the signs of when others might be trying to manipulate you enable you to intervene timeously. Additionally, if you want to build your confidence and assertiveness, then understanding manipulation is the first step towards reclaiming your power. Knowledge is empowerment, and knowing how to utilize manipulation tactics can increase your sense of agency and control.

## Segue

This chapter delved into the psychological tactics behind manipulation and shed some light on human behavior and the emotional dynamics that help you, as a woman, navigate your career and relationships effectively. Understanding frameworks like Maslow's Hierarchy of Needs and emotional triggers will equip you to not only identify, but also address the underlying motivations and vulnerabilities of people around us. This deeper awareness increases your ability to influence those around you. These insights will also help you tailor your interactions so they can help you get what you want without coming across as being manipulative. As we move forward, keep these strategies in mind to strengthen your relationships and achieve your personal goals in a balanced yet effective manner.

## Chapter 3
# COMMUNICATION STRATEGIES FOR INFLUENCE

Effective communication is one of the most powerful tools you can have in your arsenal when trying to assert control and influence. Whether showing confidence through your body language or mastering the nuances of vocal elements, understanding these techniques can make a big difference in how you are seen and how you connect with others. We will explore important aspects like body language awareness, the importance of using clear and direct language, and the art of mirroring to build rapport. Varying pitch, tone, and pacing to reinforce authority and engagement during conversations will also be discussed. By using these skills effectively, you will get all the tools needed to communicate effectively in your professional and personal settings, helping you navigate social dynamics with confidence and ease.

### Mastering Verbal and Non-Verbal Communication Skills

Mastering both verbal and non-verbal communication skills is vital when using dark manipulation. This section will give you all the tools needed to become a master manipulator.

## *Developing Verbal and Non-verbal Skills for Effective Influence*

Remember, communication is not just about what you say; it's about how you say it. The first and most important aspect of effectively communicating is being aware of your body language. Being aware of your posture, gestures, and facial expressions can make a massive difference in showing confidence. For example, standing tall with your shoulders pulled back demonstrates self-assurance, making it appear that others will take you more seriously. Using purposeful gestures while talking can help you emphasize important points, making your message more powerful. Remember, even maintaining eye contact can show sincerity and engagement. When you're interacting with someone, ensure that your facial expression is aligning with your words.

## *Vocal Aspects*

The first aspect we will discuss is the vocal aspect of communication. This includes using your pitch, tone, and pacing to reinforce your message and show your authority. For example, a steady and deliberate pace can show confidence, whereas when you speak quickly, you might show that you are nervous or uncertain. Additionally, when you change your pitch and tone, you avoid being monotonous, helping you keep the listener engaged. A lower pitch can show authority, whereas a higher pitch can come across as less commanding. You need to pay attention to your pauses so you can give the other person time to take in your message and add weight to your words. Mastering these elements enhances the influence you have in your conversations.

Clear and direct language is another important aspect of assertive communication. Demonstrate assertiveness by using straightforward speech, which helps ensure that your message is clear and understandable. For example, instead of saying, "I think we should consider trying this," go for something like, "I recommend we do this." Direct language eliminates any room for misinterpretation, and you will show yourself as someone who is decisive and confident. It's important to be clear and respectful, ensuring that you don't appear aggressive.

## *Mirroring*

Mirroring was briefly discussed in the previous chapter. It's a technique that helps you enhance the impact you have on someone. By subtly mirroring the body language of the other person, you create a sense of connection and empathy. If the person you are talking to leans forward, then you can do the same. If they are using specific hand gestures, then you can use the same ones during your conversation. Be sure not to mimic too closely, as this might come off as mocking or insincerity. The goal is to reflect the movement of the other person, which creates a subconscious bond to make them feel understood and connected while using manipulation.

By perfecting these techniques, you improve your ability to influence others. These skills can be used in professional and personal relationships and let you come across confident and assertive. Whether you're leading a meeting, negotiating a deal, or simply trying to get a desired outcome from your relationship, these skills ensure that you steer interactions toward success.

## Using Persuasive Language and Arguments

It might be overwhelming thinking about how you can use persuasive language in your arguments or during conversations. This section will help ease your anxiety by giving you valuable tips, tricks, and strategies you can use to make your interactions more effective.

### *Use the Problem-Solution-Benefit Framework*

Imagine you are about to present an important idea, or you want to get your idea across in a critical discussion. How will you organize your thoughts so they are clear and compelling? One way is by using the "problem-solution-benefit" framework. This strategy helps you clearly lay out an issue, propose a viable solution, and highlight the benefit of the solution you are discussing. This will make your argument persuasive, logical, and easier to follow.

Start by identifying the problem. For instance, you are in a meeting trying to convey why a project isn't going as expected. You should start by outlining the issue you might be facing, like lack of resources, unclear objectives, or team dynamics. Stating the problem sets the stage for your audience so they can understand the context and importance of the conversation.

Next, move on to the solution. Here's where you will give a concrete plan, addressing the problem outlined. Like if you lack resources, suggest a specific resource and how you can get it to turn things around for the project. Your solution should be attainable and practical, demonstrating your thought pattern about the problem.

Finally, highlight the benefits. This is where you should make solving the problem crystal clear. Are there positive changes your solution will bring? Will it improve productivity, morale, or profitability? By showing these benefits, you can make your argument more logical and desirable, encouraging your listener to buy into your perspective.

## *Use Rhetorical Techniques*

You can incorporate rhetorical techniques into your conversations by using metaphors, analogies, and storytelling to boost your persuasive power. Imagine you're explaining a complicated process; using a metaphor will increase its relatability. For example, comparing a business strategy to navigating a ship through stormy seas can make complex concepts more understandable and memorable. Analogies work the same as drawing parallels between known and unknown elements, helping you clarify your message.

## *Call to Action*

Creating a clear and motivational call to action is another aspect that can be very important when compiling your arguments. A call to action should be direct and inspiring, compelling your audience to act immediately. If you want your team to adopt a new tool, don't just list its features; explain how it can simplify their tasks and lead to collective success. Some of the words that might inspire your audience include "join," "start," or "lead." Ensure that your call to action is actionable and clear, leaving no room for ambiguity about what you expect to follow.

## Monitor Engagement

Looking at the verbal and non-verbal cues of your audience can give you insights on how people are reacting to your message so you can adapt it accordingly.

Monitoring how people are reacting to your message and adapting it accordingly is important to remain influential. You should look for verbal and non-verbal cues. For example, are people nodding in agreement, or do they look puzzled? When you notice they are getting disengaged, be prepared to change your approach. You might need to simplify your language, give additional examples, or address concerns directly. Flexibility in communication ensures that you keep your audience with you every step of the way. By adjusting your tone, adding a relevant joke, or asking a question, you can re-engage the audience, making your overall message more impactful.

## Active Listening and Observing Micro-Expressions

Effective communication is the cornerstone of increasing the influence you have in your relationships and one of the most important aspects to master is active listening. Active listening involves more than just hearing what the other person is saying; it requires fully engaging with the speaker, understanding their message, and responding thoughtfully. This practice helps you validate the feelings of others, establishing trust, and creating meaningful connections.

## Reflective Listening

One of the most effective active listening techniques is reflective listening. This involves paraphrasing or summarizing what the other person has told you to show that you're paying attention and you understand their point. For example, if someone is sharing a concern about feeling overwhelmed at work, you might say, "It sounds like you're really stressed with your current workload." This confirms that you are listening and validates their emotions. Validation is important because it reassures the person that their feelings are legitimate and acknowledged.

Reflective listening also helps you de-escalate conflict. When individuals feel heard, their defensiveness decreases, making it easier to resolve disagreements amicably. For example, during a heated debate, repeat the key points of what the other person has said to defuse tension and create a productive dialog.

## *Micro-Expressions*

Using micro-expressions can help enhance your ability to communicate effectively. They are brief, involuntary facial expressions that reveal true emotions, often without the speaker realizing it. Mastering the decoding of these fleeting expressions can give you invaluable insights into the hidden feelings of others.

Micro-expressions are very subtle, yet powerful, cues to use during conversations. A slight upward twitch of the lips might show genuine happiness, while a fleeting furrowed brow can show confusion or disagreement. By learning how to recognize these quick expressions, you can learn to respond empathetically and appropriately. This ability will also help you navigate various complex emotional landscapes and manage interpersonal interactions better.

Start learning this skill by looking at images or videos showing the different emotions and attempting to identify them. Observing how small changes in the facial muscles correspond to specific feelings. Over time, this practice helps sharpen your observational skills, making you better equipped to read underlying emotions during conversations.

## *Comforting Environments*

Creating environments where everyone feels comfortable sharing their thoughts and feelings is an important aspect of influential communication. People are more likely to open up when they feel safe and respected in a conversation. Establishing these environments involves demonstrating empathy, maintaining eye contact, and encouraging open-ended questions.

Empathy is an important aspect when creating a supportive environment. This includes statements like, "I can see why you'd feel that way," which shows that you care about the perspective of the other person. Maintaining eye contact, on the other hand, shows attentiveness and interest, reinforcing the speaker's sense of importance. Encouraging open-ended questions like, "How did that situation make you feel?" allows the speaker to express themselves freely, leading to richer and more meaningful conversations.

It's just as important to be mindful of non-verbal feedback, including body language and voice tone. Non-verbal cues can speak louder than the words used and impact the level of comfort of the listener. Being aware of your own body language, like nodding in agreement or maintaining an open posture, can reinforce a positive and inviting atmosphere.

Furthermore, adopt your tone of voice based on the listener's level of comfort. A calm, soothing tone can make a world of difference when discussing sensitive topics, while an enthusiastic and lively tone will work better for a casual conversation. Tone modulation helps you convey sincerity and adjusts the emotional temperature of the interaction.

Knowing when to change your approach based on the listener's responses is the hallmark of a skilled communicator. Sometimes, despite your best efforts, a conversation may not go as planned. Recognizing signs of discomfort, like crossed arms or lack of eye contact, can prompt you to shift tactics. For example, if you notice the other person becoming defensive, pause and ask if there's something that is bothering them or whether they need a break.

## Tailoring Your Message to Different Audiences

Adapting your communication style based on your audience is important for exerting influence and controlling the direction of a conversation. Understanding who your audience is step one. Think of it like prepping for an important meeting; you need to know who you are talking to so you can tailor your approach. Conducting an audience analysis will help you identify what they are interested in, what they value, and their preferences, allowing you to create a message they can relate to on a deeper level.

When you understand your audience, you can change up what you say and how you say it to make a bigger impact and influence the audience to go your way. For example, if you're speaking to a group of young professionals, use modern language and references they can relate to. On the other hand, speaking to a more traditional audience requires that you use a more formal language or established norms.

When you adjust your communication style, align it with the different cultural backgrounds and communication preferences of the people you are talking to. Each culture has its own set of rules and expectations about how to communicate effectively. For example, in some cultures, direct eye contact might be a sign of confidence, while in others, it might be considered rude. Acknowledging these differences can help you adapt your style to better resonate with a diverse audience.

### *Simplifying Ideas*

Another key strategy is to simplify complex ideas. Effective communication often means breaking down complicated concepts into simpler terms without losing the point behind your ideas. Imagine explaining a technical concept to someone who doesn't have a background in the field. You will need to give them the information in a way they can understand while maintaining its core meaning. This will make your message more understandable while ensuring your audience remains engaged and follows along.

Using analogies and metaphors can help you simplify ideas. They can transform difficult concepts into more relatable and understandable ones. For example, comparing data encryption to locking something valuable in a safe can instantly make the idea easier to grasp for someone who might not know much about cybersecurity.

### *Share Stories*

Incorporating anecdotes and shared experiences is another powerful tool for connecting with your audience. Personal stories have a unique way of engaging people because they create a sense of familiarity and relatability. When you share a story, you are building an emotional bond with your audience. For example, if you're discussing leadership challenges, sharing a personal experience where you faced and overcame obstacles can inspire and motivate your audience.

Telling a story can help you bridge the gap between perspectives. This means people will be more likely to remember and relate to the message you shared when it's wrapped in a colorful, engaging, and interesting story. Anecdotes will also help you convey lessons and insights in a way that's entertaining and educational. It can help you transform abstract ideas into concrete examples that stick with your audience.

Just remember that changing your communication style doesn't mean that you need to change who you are. It's about being flexible and responsive to the needs and preferences of your audience. By doing this, you increase the likelihood of your message being received positively and acted upon. It's about finding the sweet spot where your end goals align with the needs of your audience, creating a win-win situation.

Paying attention to the cues of your audience can give you valuable feedback, allowing you to adjust your approach in real-time to maintain influence and control over the conversation.

Remember, the ultimate goal is to create a deeper connection and understanding with your audience so you can get your desired outcome. By conducting thorough audience analysis, adjusting your communication style to fit various cultural backgrounds, simplifying complex ideas, and incorporating personal anecdotes, you can enhance your ability to influence and control conversations. This approach will make you a more effective communicator and a more empathetic and adaptive person, capable of navigating various social landscapes with ease and confidence.

**Segue**

We explored various communication techniques that empower you to assert control and influence in your relationships. You now know the importance of verbal and non-verbal communication, highlighting how body language, vocal elements, and clear, direct speech can impact your interactions. Techniques like reflective listening were also discussed as an effective way to build rapport and convey empathy, making connections genuine and meaningful. These skills can help you navigate personal and professional relationships with greater confidence and authority. You got practical tools for using persuasive language, understanding micro-expressions, and tailoring messages to different audiences. These strategies are about gaining influence and creating authentic and respectful interactions. Whether you're aiming to lead a team or deepen a personal connection, these techniques improve effective communication and assertiveness.

## Chapter 4
# BUILDING EMOTIONAL INTELLIGENCE

Building your emotional intelligence is about recognizing and managing your own emotions while using dark manipulation in your daily life. This is a skill that can significantly impact your personal and professional relationships, making them more fulfilling and less prone to conflict. By understanding how our emotions work, we have a greater power to navigate complex social interactions. This chapter provides practical steps to improve emotional intelligence, including various techniques like journaling and mindfulness, which can help you become aware of your feelings and reactions. You will be guided through methods for reading and responding to emotional cues, ensuring that you communicate effectively.

Finally, we will talk about strategies for emotional regulation and resilience, giving you the tools to stay calm and composed during challenging situations. Whether you're looking to improve your workplace dynamics or use manipulation in your personal relationships, these insights will empower you to handle your emotions skillfully and confidently.

## Understanding and Managing Your Emotions

Recognizing and controlling your emotions is the cornerstone of emotional intelligence. To manage your emotions effectively, especially when practicing dark manipulation, you need to understand them first. Pinpointing your feelings will equip you to handle those emotions before they get out of control. For many women, this is an important skill for maintaining healthy relationships.

To improve your emotional intelligence, take a moment daily to ask yourself how you are feeling. Do you feel stressed, happy, anxious, or calm? Naming your emotions helps you become more aware of them, which helps you manage them. This awareness is the foundation for better interactions, and you can easily identify what triggers your emotions and how they affect your behavior and decisions. Understanding how emotions affect your daily life will help you become a master manipulator.

### *Journaling*

Journaling is a great way to start recognizing your emotions as you write down your feelings. This helps you articulate the emotions that might be buried until you explode. Use your journal to describe your mood and the situation that influences it and how you can prevent it from happening. This practice will help you see patterns and give you insights into how different situations trigger different emotional responses.

Journaling doesn't have to be a lengthy process. Start by writing down a few lines about your day. It's also not about writing beautifully; it's about being honest with yourself. For example, if you feel like you weren't recognized during a work meeting, you can write about how that made you feel. Did you feel inadequate or frustrated? By confronting these emotions on paper, you start taking control of them instead of allowing them to control you.

### *Mindfulness Practices*

This can be a great addition to improving your emotional regulation. Mindfulness involves paying attention to the present moment without judgment. It helps you become aware of your thoughts and feelings as they arise so you can manage them more effectively. Start with simple exercises like deep breathing or guided meditation. This helps you slow down your thoughts and reduces stress, making it easier to stay calm when faced with challenging situations.

Short bursts of meditation can give you the full benefits of it. Start with five minutes or focus on your breathing to help reset your emotional state. Find a quiet place, sit comfortably, and close your eyes. Take a few deep breaths in through your nose and out through your mouth. As you breathe, take note of any tension in your body and focus on releasing it. Focus on the breath as it enters your body and exits again. If you find that your mind starts to wander, gently bring it back to focus on your breathing again.

### *Ask for Feedback*

Asking for feedback from family, friends, and colleagues is another effective strategy. You might find yourself too close to your own emotions to see them clearly. This is when you can ask for outside perspectives to get valuable insights into how you can respond when faced with different situations. Speak to someone who knows you and whose opinion you can trust. Explain that you're trying to understand how you respond emotionally and ask for honest feedback from them.

Remember to remain open-minded and not get defensive about the feedback you get. It might be difficult to hear that you may overreact during certain situations or come off as being overly critical, but these insights are important to your emotional growth. Use the feedback to reflect on your behaviors and consider how you can approach similar situations differently in the future.

Emotional awareness will make you more resilient while enhancing your relationship dynamics. Once you learn to understand your emotions and manage them accordingly, you will be less likely to lash out or withdraw when faced with conflict. This is especially important when you are trying to incorporate dark manipulation tactics into your daily life. Aim to communicate effectively and create effective interactions.

## Empathy: The Key to Understanding Others

Empathy is possibly one of the most powerful tools to building emotional intelligence, and it's an essential skill for understanding and relating to others. By enhancing your empathy skills, you can improve your manipulation skills and your interpersonal relationships. Let's dive into what empathy means and how you can develop and apply it effectively.

### *Define Empathy*

Defining empathy is your first step and involves recognizing and understanding the emotions of those around you. It's not about feeling sorry for someone; it's about putting yourself in their shoes to understand their experiences and emotions. Empathy helps you build deeper connections because it gives you the opportunity to see things from someone else's perspective. Empathy can transform your personal and professional relationships.

### *Practicing Empathy*

Practicing active listening can help you build empathy. Active listening is not just hearing words; it's about paying attention to what is being said and showing that you value it. This involved keeping eye contact, nodding your head, and saying things like "I understand" or "That must have been difficult." Avoid interrupting when practicing active listening and let the other person finish what they are saying before responding. You can also paraphrase what the other person is saying to show that you understand. For example, you might say, "So, what I'm hearing is that you're feeling overwhelmed by your workload."

### *Recognizing Non-Verbal Cues*

Look beyond the spoken words when showing empathy. This means recognizing the other person's body language, facial expressions, and tone of voice to get a better look at their emotional state. For example, crossed arms can show defensiveness or discomfort, while smiling might show happiness or friendliness. Recognizing these signals will help you understand and respond to their feelings. Imagine a colleague saying they're "fine," but their slumped posture and lack of eye contact tell a different story. These discrepancies help you respond better.

## *Showing Compassion*

Compassion is another important factor associated with empathy. Empathy allows you to understand and share feelings with others, while compassion motivates you to take action to remove some of their suffering. Building your compassion can start with small acts of kindness, like checking in on a friend who seems upset and giving them assistance without them having to ask. When we practice compassion regularly, it becomes a natural part of our response to others. This helps us create a supportive environment where everyone feels valued and understood.

Compassion can be cultivated in various ways, like helping a co-worker who is struggling with a project even when you're busy. They don't always have to be grand gestures; a simple act of kindness can have a big impact on someone's day.

## **Reading and Responding to Emotional Cues**

Recognizing emotional cues is another important step in developing your emotional intelligence and improve your communication skills. Emotional cues include a slight change in someone's voice tone or something obvious, like crying or laughing. Learning to see these signs can improve your understanding of what someone may be feeling. Start paying attention to body language, facial expressions, and silence. Understanding these signs can help you respond in a way that acknowledges and shows respect to the other person's feelings.

## *Respond Appropriately*

This is another important aspect of effective communication. Once you recognize an emotional cue, decide how you will respond to it. If your friend's upset, ask an open-ended question like "How are you feeling?" instead of assuming how they are feeling. Show genuine concern and listen without interrupting. Your response should match the intensity of their emotions. For example, if someone is visibly angry, acknowledge their anger and give support by saying, "I see you're upset. Do you want to talk about it?" This is the type of response you should aim for to validate their feelings and offer them comfort.

Responding appropriately can be tricky depending on the situation, but it's an important skill to develop. Imagine a scenario where a coworker receives negative feedback, and they're upset about it. Giving them an empathetic response involves acknowledging their feelings and offering to help them find a better solution. Instead of dismissing their emotions or trying to fix the solution, try saying, "I understand this is difficult. What can we do to make it better?" This response demonstrates empathy and support to de-escalate the situation and build trust.

## *Emotional Responsiveness*

This requires that you put in consistent efforts. It's not enough to recognize and understand emotions; you need to make them part of your daily interactions. Practice during low-stakes situations first to get a significant advantage. Ask your friends and family about how their day was and listen to their answers. You can expand this to your colleagues and acquaintances. The more you practice, the more natural this exercise will become. It can help you build stronger relationships because people will see you as someone who cares about their feelings and perspectives.

As you practice emotional responsiveness, remember it's a journey. There will be times when you misread a cue or respond in an unhelpful way. These moments should be used as learning opportunities. Reflect on what you did wrong and how you can change your approach next time. Journaling can also help you keep track of your interactions. Write down situations where you successfully recognized and responded to someone's emotions, and times when things didn't go well. This reflection will help you identify patterns where you can improve your emotional intelligence.

## Create a Feedback Loop

This is another effective strategy for assessing your emotional responses to improve your personal growth. After responding to the emotional state of someone else, take a look at how they react to your response. Did they calm down? Did they open up? Or did they become withdrawn? Use these observations to refine your approach and ask for direct feedback when needed. For example, after a tough conversation, you can ask, "I hope I handled that well. How did you feel about our discussion?" Constructive feedback gives you insights into how you can improve your emotional responses in the conversations you have.

The feedback loop isn't just about receiving feedback from others; it involves self-assessment. After an interaction, take a moment to reflect on your emotions. Were you calm and supportive, or did you let your own feelings cloud your response? Self-awareness is a key component of emotional intelligence. By understanding your emotional triggers, you can manage them and respond to others more effectively.

Understanding how to decode and respond to emotional cues helps improve your interpersonal relationships and is invaluable in professional settings. In a work environment, recognizing when a colleague is stressed and offering support can create a collaborative and positive environment. It shows that you're attentive and considerate, which helps improve teamwork and productivity. Moreover, showing higher emotional intelligence, you will become more approachable and trustworthy, making it easier for team members to communicate openly and for you to use dark manipulation techniques to get your way.

Remember, there will be times when you misread a cue or respond unhelpfully. These moments should be learning opportunities where you should reflect on what you did wrong and how you can change next time. Journaling can be beneficial and help you keep track of where you went wrong. Write down where you successfully recognized and responded to someone's emotions and where things didn't go as expected. This reflection will help you identify patterns where you can improve your emotional intelligence over time.

Incorporating these skills into your daily life helps you to transform your relationships. People are drawn to people who show empathy and understanding. Showing that you care helps you create an environment of trust and mutual respect. This strengthens your personal bonds and enhances your professional reputation.

## Techniques for Emotional Regulation and Resilience

Managing your emotions can feel like taming a whirlwind. But when you put practical strategies in place, you can navigate this emotional landscape effectively. This section will explore techniques that might become your go-to tools for emotional regulation and resilience.

### *Breathing Exercises*

Breathing exercises is the first technique to help you with your emotional regulation. Breathing is not only about surviving; it's a powerful way to take control of your emotional state. Deep breathing helps you slow down your heart rate and clear your mind, making it easier for you to manage your stress and anxiety levels. The most popular technique is the 4-7-8 technique, where you inhale through your nose for four seconds, hold for seven seconds, and then exhale slowly through your mouth for eight seconds. Repeat this exercise as many times as you need to get yourself centered. This technique also helps activate your parasympathetic nervous system, so you feel more relaxed. Taking a few moments to focus on your breath makes the world of difference when you feel overwhelmed.

### *Reframing Your Thoughts*

Reframing your thoughts requires you to change the way you view various situations to change your emotional responses. For example, if you're facing a challenging project at work, then instead of thinking, "This is too hard; I can't do it," change your mindset to, "This is an opportunity for me to learn and grow." Doing this helps reduce negative feelings and helps you approach challenges with a positive mindset. It's not about ignoring difficulties; instead, you will see them in a new light. Practicing this technique can enhance your overall emotional well-being.

## Building Resilience

It's important to understand that adversity can be a powerful tool when building resilience. Life throws various challenges at us, and how we respond can show the resilience we have. Building resilience doesn't mean avoiding or denying hardships; it's about facing them head-on and learning from them. Consider a difficult situation you encountered in the past. How did you handle it? What did you learn from it? Reflecting on these experiences helps you see your strengths and where you can improve. As time goes by, you'll develop a stronger sense of self and a greater ability to bounce back from setbacks.

## Self-Care

Prioritizing self-care is another important factor in maintaining your emotional health. Taking care of yourself isn't selfish; it's about maintaining your mental and emotional stability. Adding self-care practices to your routine gives you a solid foundation for managing stress and enhancing your well-being. Self-care comes in many forms, including physical activity, nutrition, and mental and emotional practices. Look for the practices that work for you by listening to your body and mind and giving yourself time to rest and recharge when you need it.

Let's put all these strategies together. Imagine a tough day at work. Start by taking a few deep breaths to calm yourself down. Once you feel calmer, attempt to refrain from the situation. Instead of focusing on the stress, think about what you can learn from the experience. Maybe you can use the experience to improve your skills or relationships with your colleagues. Remember, this challenge can be used as an opportunity to strengthen your resilience too. Finally, treat yourself to self-care practices after a long day at work, whether it's a relaxing bath, a walk in nature, or a good book. These practices will make you better equipped to handle whatever comes next.

Remember, managing your emotions takes time. Be patient with yourself and keep practicing the techniques mentioned in this chapter. Over time, you'll find that you can navigate your emotions and maintain your sense of balance, even when facing challenges. Whether using breathing exercises, cognitive reframing, building resilience, or practicing self-care, each strategy will contribute to a healthier, more emotionally intelligent you.

You will notice an improvement in how you handle stress and interact with others when you implement these strategies. Emotional intelligence isn't just about understanding your emotions; it's about recognizing and responding to the emotions of others. Becoming more adept at managing your feelings, you'll find your relationships improving and feel more empowered in your personal and professional life.

Remember, there will always be new challenges and opportunities for growth. Embrace them with an open mind and compassionate heart. Doing this will improve your emotional well-being while creating a positive ripple effect in your relationships.

The strategies mentioned here are just the beginning. Continue exploring and practicing different techniques to find what works for you. Stay curious and be kind to yourself. Your emotional health is worth the effort, and the benefits go far beyond your own well-being.

**Segue**

This chapter provided tools to help you enhance your emotional intelligence, helping you understand and manage your own emotions before trying to use other people's emotions against them. By recognizing what you're feeling and using techniques like journaling and mindfulness, you can navigate your emotional landscape. These practices will help make you more resilient while helping you interact with others. As you continue to apply these strategies, remember that it's a continuous journey. Reflect on your emotions regularly and seek feedback from trusted friends and colleagues to help refine your skills. With time and practice, you'll become more equipped to handle your own feelings and those of others, empowering you to build stronger connections personally and professionally.

## Chapter 5

# ASSERTIVE LEADERSHIP IN PERSONAL RELATIONSHIPS

Taking the lead in your personal relationships is another aspect of empowering yourself as a woman. By understanding and implementing key strategies, you create healthier dynamics and build a foundation where others won't see you as being manipulative.

This chapter will discuss essential topics to help you navigate the complex topic of interpersonal communication, ensuring that your needs are met while maintaining harmony. I will give you practical steps to setting and maintaining boundaries, which are important for creating balanced relationships. You will learn about creating transformative conversations with your partner, ensuring that your discussions will go your way. You will also get insights into effectively handling conflicts and turning disagreements into learning opportunities. Mastering these skills will equip you to lead with effectiveness.

**Setting Boundaries and Sticking to Them**

Setting boundaries is an important aspect of life. It holds true, especially with personal relationships. Look at boundaries as invisible lines that help you define where you end and where others begin. They help protect your physical space, emotions, thoughts, and needs. Understanding the personal boundaries you need to protect is the first step to creating respectful and healthy relationships. Look at your limits and distinguish what you can tolerate and what makes you uncomfortable or stressed.

## *Creating Your Boundaries*

Establishing boundaries is the foundation that shows respect and trust in your relationships. Take time to understand your own limits to become better equipped to communicate them clearly to others. Knowing when to say "no" and being comfortable with your decision can prevent resentment while improving your self-respect. For example, if you need time to recharge, then communicate this need so you aren't overwhelmed by constant social interactions. This awareness helps you avoid situations that may impose on your comfort zones, allowing your relationships to grow on mutual consent and understanding.

## *Communicating Your Boundaries*

Communicating the boundaries you set is another important skill. Simply knowing what your limits are isn't enough; you need to express them clearly. Be honest about what you want and need from your relationships and use "I" statements to set your boundaries. For example, instead of saying, "You always interrupt me," try, "I don't feel heard when I am being interrupted during conversations." This approach will focus on your own feelings instead of blaming others. This ensures that your boundaries are understood and respected.

Remember to stay calm when communicating your boundaries with others. Avoid raising your voice or getting defensive to avoid any misunderstandings or conflicts. Instead, be clear, concise, and firm about what your needs are. If someone reacts negatively to your boundaries, remain firm. You need to show that you are serious about the boundaries you are setting.

## Maintaining Your Boundaries

Maintaining your boundaries may seem challenging, especially when facing resistance and external pressure. The key is to stay consistent. Hold on to your boundaries regardless of the situation. When you start making exceptions, you confuse others and undermine your efforts. Being consistent show that your boundaries are important, and you're telling others that they need to be taken seriously.

Remind yourself why you set boundaries if you want to maintain them. Reflect on past experiences when you didn't have boundaries and how it caused discomfort and stress. These experiences can help you stay committed to your limits. You can also practice self-care to ensure that you have the mental and emotional strength to enforce your boundaries. This includes setting time aside for activities you enjoy, seeking support from friends, and engaging in mindfulness practices.

Anticipating challenges can also be helpful. Consider scenarios where your boundaries will be tested and prepare your responses in advance. For example, if your friend calls you late at night and disrupts your sleep, then plan ahead on how you can handle it. Turn your phone to silent or set a clear boundary about the cut-off time you have for calls. By planning ahead, you reduce the likelihood of putting your boundaries at risk.

## Recognize the Signs

By training yourself to recognize the signs of your boundaries being violated, you prepare yourself to manage them. There might be times when your boundaries are crossed without you noticing, making it difficult to identify the issue. Pay attention to your emotional and physical state, like feeling uncomfortable, resentment, or anxious. These are signs that your boundaries are not being respected. Physical signs also include tension, fatigue, or headaches, which are signs your body gives to warn you of violations.

Note the behaviors of others. Are they ignoring your boundaries? Do they guilt-trip or manipulate you into doing things against your will?

These are signs that your boundaries are being crossed and they should be addressed immediately. Let the person know that their actions are affecting you and remind them of your boundaries. For example, you might say, "I felt uncomfortable when you pressured me to stay late. I need to stick to my agreed-upon schedule."

Remember, it's not just about reacting when your boundaries are being violated; it's about informing others about your boundaries. People might cross them without knowing about them. If this is the case, gently tell them about your limits to create understanding and cooperation with those around you. For example, after the initial conversation about your discomfort, follow up with examples or reminders if your boundaries are crossed again.

## Balancing Assertiveness With Compassion

You need to balance your assertiveness with empathy in order to create strong, healthy dynamics where you can use that to your advantage. This is an art that requires understanding the nuances of communication and behavior. Let's take a look at how you can achieve this balance effectively.

### *Understanding Assertiveness vs. Aggression*

Distinguishing between assertiveness and aggression will be the first topic. Assertiveness is expressing your feelings, needs, and boundaries with confidence and respect. It's about standing up for yourself without being disrespectful towards others. Aggression, on the other hand, disregards the feelings and rights of other people, which leads to hostility and conflict. This distinction is key to ensuring that your assertiveness is positively received, as opposed to causing unnecessary tension.

Imagine asking your partner to help you with household chores. An assertive approach would be calmly explaining why their assistance is needed. Say something like, "I am feeling overwhelmed with how chores are divided. We should discuss a fairer way to share these responsibilities." This can be contrasted with an aggressive statement: "You never help me around the house! Why are you so lazy?" The latter is likely to get a defensive reaction and cause conflict, where the first invites a constructive conversation and increases your chance of manipulating your partner to get what you need.

## Using Compassion in Conflict

Tackling conflicts with compassion helps you transform potentially negative interactions into opportunities for growth and connection. When you encounter disagreements, it's easy to get caught up in frustration and forget the importance of staying kind. However, using compassion can de-escalate tensions and create a path for resolution.

For example, when having a disagreement about finances that turns ugly, instead of letting your anger dominate the conversation, acknowledge the feelings you both have, including your partner's concerns. You might say, "I understand that money stresses you out, and I feel the same way. Let's work together to find a solution." This approach shows that you care about their well-being and the health of your relationship, which leads to a more productive discussion and outcome.

Taking breaks during heated arguments can be an act of compassion. If things get intense, suggest pausing the discussion until both of you have calmed down. This prevents hurtful words from being said and allows you to have a clear, more empathetic conversation later.

## Assessing the Right Moments

Knowing when to use compassion instead of assertiveness is a powerful skill that requires practice and self-awareness. Not every situation will call for the same approach, and part of being assertive is recognizing which strategy to use during a specific situation.

When you facing situations where your boundaries are being repeatedly crossed, stronger assertiveness might be needed. For example, if you've politely asked your partner multiple times to be quiet during your working hours and they continue to interrupt you, then it might be time to assert yourself more firmly. You could say, "I understand that you want to spend time with me, but I need uninterrupted focus during my working hours. Can we agree on specific times to talk?"

There might be times when you need to be more compassionate. If your partner is going through a tough time, then showing extra empathy and understanding can strengthen your connection. You might prioritize listening and supporting them over addressing less urgent issues.

You can keep the "three strikes" rule in mind when doing this: if you've addressed an issue three times without seeing a change, then it might be time to escalate your level of assertiveness. However, ensure that your communication is respectful and considerate.

## Transformative Conversations With Partners

Having intentions behind your conversations is equally important when using manipulation and strengthening your personal relationships. Before communicating with your partner, prepare yourself mentally so you can get the outcome you want. This means taking a moment to think about what you want to achieve. Visualize the outcome you want and consider the best way to speak your mind. This ensures that you maintain focus and clarity throughout the conversation.

### *Ask Yourself Questions*

Asking yourself a few questions before setting intentions is a critical part. Some of these questions include:

- What's the purpose of the conversation?
- What are my goals?
- What do I want my partner to feel at the end of the discussion?

The answers to these questions will give you a clearer understanding of your objectives, which helps guide your conversation towards a productive conclusion. It also reduces the chances of misunderstandings or emotional flare-ups, making the entire process go smoother.

## Creating Safe Dialogue

This is another important aspect for conversations to be transformative, as both parties need to feel comfortable and open. Choose the right time and place to start your conversation and ensure that it's free from distractions and interruptions. No one wants to talk while multitasking or dealing with background noise.

## Use Your Body Language

Your body language should be open; this includes gestures like eye contact, nodding, and leaning forward to show that you're fully engaged and supportive. Reassure your partner that you value their thoughts and feelings by using phrases like "I understand" or "I see where you're coming from." This helps create trust and encourages your partner to express themselves.

Navigating difficult topics can be challenging, but it's important for building strong relationships. When discussing sensitive topics, acknowledge the difficulty by using phrases like "I know this is hard to talk about" to help relieve tension.

Maintaining a calm and steady tone of voice is also important. This means avoiding blaming the other person and not using accusatory language. Instead, use "I" statements to express your feelings and perspectives.

It might be helpful to break down bigger issues into smaller, more manageable parts. This will help you resolve the issues effectively before moving on to the next one. This will prevent conversations from becoming overwhelming while ensuring that important topics are discussed.

## Follow-up and Accountability

Another important aspect of productive conversations is following up. You need to take time after a conversation to recap on the main points and agreements made. This helps reinforce a mutual understanding and commitment to the decisions agreed upon.

Set aside time to review your conversations and discuss any new concerns. This will show your partner that you're dedicated to resolving issues and improving your relationships even more. It will also give you the opportunity to celebrate positive changes that happened, and you can check the pending areas.

Both of you need to be held accountable for following through with the commitments you made in your relationship. Discuss any issues that arise when one of you fails to uphold your end of the deal. Not having these discussions can cause resentment and trust to be broken over time.

**Strategies for Handling Conflict Effectively**

When it comes to resolving conflicts, you need to recognize its nature. You might look at conflict as negative, but understand that conflict is a natural part of any relationship. You might experience conflict due to varying opinions, needs, or desires. This doesn't mean that your relationship is failing; instead, it gives you an opportunity to grow and get a deeper understanding of your partner. Understanding that conflicts may happen will help you stay calm and have a proactive mindset when it happens instead of avoiding or fearing them. Let's take a look at some conflict resolution skills.

*Effective Communication*

Once again, communication is an important aspect of your relationships. Another effective strategy (as mentioned before) is using "I" statements when confronted with conflict. You can start practicing mindfulness techniques during disagreements, so your emotions aren't boiling over. Take deep breaths, maintain eye contact, and take notice of your body language and tone to ensure that you stay neutral and non-threatening.

*Compromising*

Knowing when to compromise is another important skill when attempting to navigate conflicts. Flexibility when handling conflicts can make all the difference. It's important to recognize that not all disagreements have a clear winner or loser. Sometimes, finding a middle ground is where both parties make concessions that lead to a better outcome. Compromise shouldn't be viewed as giving up on your needs but rather as making adjustments for mutual benefit. For example, if you're arguing about spending weekends with family versus spending time alone, consider alternating weekend and splitting time. When both parties feel heard and valued, the foundation of your relationships gets stronger.

Learning from conflicts will help you address disputes in your relationships. Every conflict you're part of gives you valuable insights into your partner's personality, your own triggers, and the dynamics of your relationship. After your conflict has been resolved, take a moment to reflect on what happened. What triggered the disagreement? How did you respond? Could the conflicts have been avoided or handled differently? Discuss these reflections openly with your partner to get mutual understanding and improve future interactions. By analyzing past disputes, you can build a toolkit of strategies that helps you navigate future conflicts more effectively.

**Segue**

Taking charge of your personal relationships involves various things, including setting firm boundaries while nurturing open and honest conversations. This chapter showed you how important it is for you to define your limits clearly and communicate them assertively without using aggression. By understanding and respecting your own boundaries, you create healthier and more respectful interactions while avoiding misunderstanding and resentment. Consistency and self-care also play an important role in maintaining these boundaries, ensuring they are upheld during difficult situations. You should also balance assertiveness with empathy to communicate effectively and resolve conflicts effectively. Assertiveness helps in putting your needs forward clearly while transforming conflicts into opportunities for mutual growth and understanding. Preparing for conversations, creating safe spaces, and navigating difficult topics with compassion helps you reclaim your power and fosters relationships built on mutual respect and cooperation.

## Chapter 6
# LEVERAGING FEMININITY AS POWER

Your femininity is one of the most powerful things you have when using dark manipulation strategies. Learning how to leverage it encourages you to embrace qualities traditionally seen as feminine and using them in your personal and professional lives. By defining traits like empathy, nurturing, and vulnerability, you can transform perceived weaknesses into unique strengths.

This chapter will show you how modern female leaders are using their femininity to influence others and assert their presence. You will get practical ways to harness your feminine qualities to command respect and build influential relationships. We'll explore the significance of empathy and nurturing in leadership roles, emphasizing how these attributes can increase team cohesion and effective communication. We'll also look at examples of successful women who leveraged their femininity to navigate challenging situations and come out stronger. From everyday professional scenarios to high-stakes negotiations, this chapter will give you actionable insights into how women can turn their femininity into an amazing force.

**Breaking Down Misconceptions About Femininity**

There are various traits associated with femininity that are often misunderstood and undervalued. This section will uncover each of them and what makes them valuable as a female using dark manipulation strategies.

## *Empathy and Nurturing*

Many believe that traits associated with femininity, like empathy and nurturing, are signs of weakness. However, these qualities are powerful leadership assets. Empathy allows you to understand your team members' needs and motivations, fostering a supportive environment where everyone feels valued. This understanding leads to more effective communication and stronger, more cohesive teams. Nurturing can involve guiding and supporting others towards their best selves, which is essential for good leadership.

## *Vulnerability*

Vulnerability is often overlooked as a source of strength. Showing your vulnerability creates an atmosphere of trust and authenticity. Your team members will feel safe to express their thoughts and ideas, leading to more innovative solutions and better outcomes. Brene Brown, a researcher on vulnerability, emphasizes that embracing vulnerability creates deeper connections and drives courage. By reframing vulnerability as a strength, you can use this weakness to your advantage, enhancing your influence and effectiveness in any situation.

## *Embracing Your Unique Characteristics*

Recognizing how femininity is misjudged gives you an opportunity to redefine it on your terms. Instead of conforming to societal expectations, embrace your unique characteristics and use them strategically. For example, consider the nurturing aspect of femininity as caring and a strategic asset for mentoring and developing talent within your organization. See yourself through the lens so you can gain confidence in your abilities and project confidence, influencing perceptions and challenging stereotypes.

## *Celebrating Approaches*

Celebrating feminine approaches to leadership involves acknowledging and valuing these unique strengths. Instead of trying to fit into the mold created by male-dominated leadership paradigms, highlight your distinctive qualities. There are various stories of successful female leaders who leverage their empathy, vulnerability, and nurturing natures as essential in the modern world. Companies and teams benefit from diverse leadership styles and the inclusion of feminine qualities to have a more balanced and thoughtful decision-making process.

An excellent example of this concept is Jacinda Ardern, the Prime Minister of New Zealand. her leadership during crises, such as the Christchurch Mosque shooting and the COVID-19 pandemic, demonstrated how empathy and clear, compassionate communication could unite a nation and give a sense of security. By being herself and leveraging her feminine qualities, Ardern showed the world that there is immense power in what had traditionally been seen as "soft" leadership skills (Lau, 2023).

## *Understanding These Elements*

It's equally important to understand how to apply these elements practically. In everyday professional scenarios, you can use your empathetic nature to mediate conflicts, build consensus, and encourage a more collaborative nature. During negotiations, showing vulnerability by acknowledging uncertainties can disarm opponents and pave the way for more honest, productive dialogues. These strategies can demonstrate how feminine qualities are far from weakness. They are strengths that, when used correctly, command respect and drive success.

## *Provide Support*

While on your journey to embracing your femininity as power, remember to support each other. Mentorship and networks among women can amplify these efforts, providing a platform for shared experiences and collective growth. Mentoring others lets you pass along your knowledge and skills while understanding that femininity can be a strength. This creates a ripple effect, empowering more women to step into leadership roles with confidence and authenticity.

This means that misjudging femininity can be seen as an opportunity to redefine and celebrate your unique approach to leadership. You can challenge stereotypes and reshape societal norms. Leadership doesn't need to be a one-size-fits-all model. The future of effective leadership lies in diversity—in recognizing and valuing different styles and approaches, including those rooted in femininity.

## Combining Grace With Strength

To use your power of femininity, it's important to strike a balance between grace and inner strength. This blend creates a compelling presence that influences and commands respect in various situations. Let's look at how this integration works and see practical ways to develop them.

### *Grace in Communication*

Firstly, we will look at grace in communication and interaction. Grace isn't just about being elegant and poised; it's about how you carry yourself and engage others with kindness and understanding. This practice involves active listening, showing empathy, and responding thoughtfully. Communicating gracefully helps you create a space where others feel heard and valued, which leads to positive and productive interactions.

On the other hand, inner strength will encompass assertiveness without aggression. Being strong doesn't mean being harsh and domineering. It's about expressing your opinions and needs confidently while still respecting others. Inner strength helps you set and maintain boundaries, making it clear that while you value the perspectives of others, your own thoughts and feelings are also important.

## *Integrating Strength and Grace*

This might seem tricky, but can be developed through practical exercise. One effective method is role-playing various scenarios where you practice asserting your views gracefully. For example, imagine you're in a meeting where your ideas are being challenged. Instead of reacting defensively, take a breath, listen actively, and respond with a calm, firm tone. Doing this helps you blend assertiveness with grace over time.

## *Meditation*

Mindfulness meditation is very useful. It helps you develop self-awareness and emotional regulation, which is important for maintaining grace under pressure and staying strong without becoming aggressive. Spend a few minutes daily focusing on your breath and observing your thoughts without judgment. This habit enforces your ability to respond thoughtfully instead of impulsively.

## *Learn From Others*

The decision-making and interpersonal interactions of other leaders who use grace can give you valuable insights. Michele Obama is a great example. Her speeches highlight her ability to address critical issues assertively while maintaining a compassionate and approachable demeanor. Her graceful communication style, with a strong stance on important topics, has earned her respect and admiration from people around the world.

## *Practical Examples*

Practical examples can also show you how combining grace, and strength can transform your professional and personal relationships. Consider negotiating a raise at work. Approaching this situation with assertiveness might come off as demanding, whereas when you use grace, your needs might not be seen. A balanced approach involves clearly stating your contributions and the justification for your raise while acknowledging the standpoint of the company. This combination shows that you're confident in your worth, but you're also considerate of the organization's position.

This balance helps you resolve conflicts in your personal relationships. For example, when having a disagreement with a friend, responding with grace means listening and validating their feelings. Incorporating strength involves standing firm on your perspectives if it's important to you. Doing this means that you're respecting their viewpoint while respecting your values.

## Find Specific Activities

To help you build these qualities, start looking for specific activities where you can use both aspects. These include public speaking or debate clubs to help you improve your assertive communication skills and allow you to present your ideas confidently. Participating in yoga or theatre can enhance your bodily awareness and expressive capabilities, contributing to a graceful demeanor.

Remember, using your femininity as a power doesn't mean you need to abandon who you are. It's about embracing the most powerful facets of yourself—your gentleness, assertiveness, empathy, and toughness—and knowing when and how to use these qualities to your advantage. The key is to find harmony in how you present yourself when communicating with others.

## Using Charm as a Strategic Tool

Your charm is powerful in building relationships while influencing others. By understanding the various components of charm and how to incorporate them into your daily conversations allows you to create positive connections and build mutual respect. Let's dive into what charm is and how you can use it to enhance your personal and professional life.

## Elements of Charm

There are essentially several key elements of charm, including kindness and charisma. Kindness is being considerate and empathetic towards others, creating a warm and welcoming environment. It's about caring for people and showing you care through both your actions and words. Charisma, on the other hand, is the magnetism and appeal you use to draw people to you. Charisma is seen in people who are confident, enthusiastic, and able to communicate with ease. When combined, kindness and charisma make up the essence of charm, making you more approachable and likable.

*Incorporation Tips*

There are various tips you can use to incorporate charm into your daily interactions to help you build stronger relationships. These include:

**Active Listening:** Active listening has been discussed various times, and it's just as important when using your charm to get your desired outcome. Aim to maintain your eye contact during conversations to show your confidence and interest in conversations.

**Body Language:** Your charm increases when you use positive body language with it. This includes open gestures like smiling and having a relaxed posture to look more inviting. Other people will be drawn to you when you display warmth and positivity.

**Compliment Others:** Compliment the other person to increase your charm. Genuine compliments lift others up and create a positive atmosphere, making them feel appreciated and valued.

**Stay Funny:** Humor plays a big role in charm. Using well-timed jokes or light-hearted comments to break the ice and make your interactions more enjoyable. However, it's important to be mindful of the context and ensure your humor is appropriate and inclusive.

**Be Open and Vulnerable:** This is another important aspect to enhance your charm. Sharing your personal stories or admitting to mistakes you make can make you relatable and seem more human in the eyes of others. Vulnerability fosters authenticity, which is crucial for building genuine connections. When people see you're willing to be open and honest, they'll be more likely to do the same, leading to deeper and more meaningful relationships.

## Defusing Tension

One advantage of using your charm is defusing tension during difficult situations. When facing conflict or disagreements, use your charm to calm emotions and open up communication lines. For example, approaching a heated discussion with a calm and friendly demeanor can prevent situations from getting escalated. Showing empathy and understanding helps others feel heard and respected, even with differing opinions.

## Real-Life Examples

Let's take a look at some real-life examples to help illustrate how powerful these points are.

Imagine negotiating with a colleague in a professional setting. Approaching them with kindness and charisma helps you set a positive tone. Listen to their concerns and maintain eye contact to show you're paying attention. Use positive body language and offer sincere compliments to build rapport. Use humor to lighten tension that might build. Share your own challenges and encourage your colleagues to share their perspectives, paving the way for collaborative solutions. Then turn any situation to give you the outcome you want by using dark manipulation strategies. The key is to make the person you're manipulating comfortable before getting them to do what you want.

Imagine resolving a disagreement with a friend in a personal setting. Instead of reacting defensively, approach the conversation with empathy and understanding. Acknowledge their feelings and express your feelings calmly and kindly. Use your charm to de-escalate the situation and lead to a more constructive dialogue. Share vulnerable moments or past experiences related to the issue you're experiencing to create a deeper connection and show you're invested in the relationship.

Using your charm in everyday interactions doesn't mean you're being insincere or manipulative. It's about finding the balance between being kind, charismatic, and authentic. Charm should enhance your natural personality and reflect your true self. Using your charm strategically can be a powerful tool to build relationships, influence others effectively, and create a positive impact on your personal and professional life.

## Maintaining Authenticity While Asserting Power

Staying authentic is important when using your femininity as a source of power and influence. It ensures your assertiveness feels genuine and resonant, making it impactful and sustainable. This section discusses the importance of being authentic, giving you practical advice on how you can express yourself while maintaining who you truly are.

### *Self-Awareness*

Self-awareness is an important part of authenticity. This means having a clear understanding of your personality, including your strengths, weaknesses, thoughts, beliefs, motivations, and emotions. Being self-aware allows you to stay true to yourself while interacting with others. Knowing who you are and what you stand for helps guide your actions and decisions, making them feel natural rather than forced. To build your self-awareness, you can regularly reflect on your experiences and feelings. This can be done through journaling, meditation, or talking to a trusted friend.

### *Strategies to Express Yourself*

There are various strategies to help you express your thoughts and feelings while staying authentic to who you are. These include being honest, using "I" statements, communicating assertively, and practicing active listening.

Understanding how you can assert your power without losing your true self is important in this section. You might feel pressured to adopt behaviors that seem authoritative, but they might not align with your natural disposition. Remember, true power comes from within, and it's amplified when you stay true to yourself. Consider the cultural symbols of femininity, including traits like compassion, empathy, and nurturing. These qualities are often undervalued in traditional power structures, but they can be used along with your dark manipulation strategies to get your desired outcomes. For example, empathetic leadership can encourage team cohesion and loyalty, which can be useful in a professional setting. You don't have to shed your feminine traits to assert power; you can use them to your advantage instead, turning them into a unique strength.

## *Building Relationships*

Being authentic helps build sustainable relationships and increases loyalty and respect from others. Authentic interactions act as the foundation of meaningful relationships because they create mutual respect and understanding. For example, when you consistently act according to your values. Your team will start respecting you for your decisions and your integrity. This respect translates to loyalty, because your team members will feel valued and understood. The same goes for personal relationships because your partner will be more open and supportive, strengthening your bond with them.

One great example is using cultural symbols of femininity for personal empowerment. Throughout various societies, symbols of femininity like grace, beauty, and emotional intelligence have a significant cultural impact. You can use these symbols authentically to create your own version of power. For example, showing your emotional intelligence during workplace negotiations or employing graceful dialogue when faced with challenging social situations shows how these attributes can be powerful tools for using dark manipulation.

Delving into authenticity, it's important to remember that it doesn't lead to being perfect. Authenticity requires acknowledging and accepting imperfections. Embracing your flaws can be incredibly empowering because it frees you from the constant pressures of needing to be perfect. In turn, this acceptance can make it easier for you to connect with others because they'll feel more comfortable around someone who is genuinely human and relatable.

Practical steps to maintaining authenticity include setting boundaries, practicing self-care, and aligning your actions with your core values. Setting boundaries ensures that you're not overextending yourself or compromising your values to please others. Self-care, like getting rest, eating healthy, and taking mental health breaks, is important for maintaining your energy and clarity so you can act authentically. Continuously revisiting and aligning your actions with your core values helps keep you grounded in your true self.

## Segue

This chapter explored how you can embrace your femininity as a unique strength to influence others and gain respect in various relationships and settings. Redefining traditional perceptions about traits like empathy, nurturing, and vulnerability, you can use them as powerful leadership tools. These qualities help you create deeper connections, better communication, and effective team dynamics. Leveraging these strengths can challenge stereotypes and reshape societal norms, demonstrating that feminine approaches are valuable and essential in your personal and professional life. Going forward, find a balance between grace and strength and know when to sue each wisely. This can be through empathetic listening, assertive yet kind interactions, or integrating charm into your daily life. These traits can transform how you navigate life. Embrace your authentic self while maintaining your power shows that true strength comes from within, and use this knowledge to encourage more women to lead with confidence and authenticity.

## Chapter 7

# DEVELOPING A STRATEGIST'S MINDSET

Developing a strategist's mindset is important for getting what you want in your personal and professional life. It involves understanding your core values, defining specific objectives, visualizing your desired outcomes, and creating a plan of action. By incorporating these elements, you can navigate difficult situations with confidence and poise. This chapter will give you practical strategies to help empower you to make informed decisions, adapt to changing situations, and maintain ethical integrity. You will learn about the importance of identifying your core values to stay true to yourself in all your actions. We'll discuss setting SMART goals, which will help guide your efforts effectively. We'll also look at visualization techniques to help you connect with your goals and boost your confidence. Finally, we'll discuss purposeful strategies that break down your objectives into manageable steps.

## Identifying Your Goals and Desired Outcomes

This section will look at various aspects of your core values and how they relate to your specific goals. Let's dive into this important topic and how to use it to your advantage when using dark manipulation.

### *Understanding Your Core Values*

Before diving into manipulation, it's important to understand your core values. Having strong core values means that your actions will align with who you are. This ensures authenticity, which is important for your personal integrity and long-term success. Without strong core values guiding your decisions, your manipulation strategies can quickly become unethical and harm your relationships and reputation.

Having a clear idea of what matters to you makes it easier to navigate complex situations. Instead of being swayed by short-term gains, your decisions are rooted in understanding your long-term goals and objectives. For example, any manipulative act must align with that, ensuring that you're not deceitful and, instead, strategic.

### *Defining Specific Goals*

After establishing your core values, your next steps are to define clear and measurable goals. When your goals are specific, they'll help your focus and efforts be more direct. You can use the SMART goal criteria here. This stands for Specific, Measurable, Achievable, Realistic, and Timely. These goals help increase your motivation because you'll know exactly what you're aiming for, and it'll help you measure your progress along the way.

Imagine navigating relationships where you wish to have more influence. Instead of just being more influential," break it down. Do you want to be consulted on important decisions? Do you want to lead conversations? These are specific goals to guide your manipulative strategies effectively.

## Visualizing Desired Outcomes

Visualization is a powerful tool to achieving your goals, including when employing manipulation tactics. By picturing your outcomes, you can create a deeper connection to the results you want. Visualization shows you what success will look like, making it easier for you to recognize when you achieve it. Additionally, visualizing successful scenarios builds confidence in dark manipulation strategies.

Think about this: Visualize yourself successfully leading a team project. This mental practice will prepare you for the real-life situation, which gives you the ability to perform confidently and decisively.

For example, visualize a scenario where your dark manipulation strategies have led you to a promotion. Picture the congratulatory message, the new office, and the added responsibilities. This image will make the goal appear more tangible and create the belief that achieving it is within your grasp. It can significantly increase your self-confidence and drive, both essential elements in the realm of dark manipulation.

## Outlining Purposeful Strategies

After setting goals and visualizing your outcomes, it's time to outline your strategies. Outlining these strategies involves breaking down your goals into manageable steps and aligning your actions with overarching objectives. This helps you simplify the process and reduces decision fatigue because you will have a clear plan in place.

For example, if your goal is to get a leadership role at work through dark manipulation, then you can list the steps you need to take. Including building relationships with higher management first, demonstrating your skills through smaller projects, or subtly positioning yourself as a key member of the team. By laying out these steps, your goal becomes clearer and more achievable.

Understanding strong core values ensures that you're authentic in your actions, which will reinforce long-term success over short-term gains. Having solid core values ensures that your actions are more likely to be perceived as genuine, building trust even with manipulation. This trust is invaluable because it creates a foundation of loyalty and respect that paves the way for you to influence people.

Your core values will help keep you grounded and give you a point of reference during difficult or morally ambiguous situations. They remind you of the reasons for your goals and help you stay true to yourself, reducing the risk of falling into unethical behavior that could lead to unsuccessful outcomes.

Now it's time to craft a detailed and actionable plan, including clear and measurable goals, which will act as milestones to gauge your progress and keep you accountable towards your constant progress. Metrics like deadlines, specific tasks, and performance indicators help keep your plan on track. These details will also keep you focused and committed to achieving your goals.

If you want to boost your influence in the workplace within six months, then you might want to break this goal down. For example, you can add attending networking events bi-weekly, volunteering for high-visibility projects monthly, and seeking feedback from mentors quarterly. These smaller goals help you stay focused and motivated, giving you clear checkpoints to assess your progress.

For example, if your strategies involve gaining favor with influential peers in your workplace, your plan can include tailored steps like learning about their interests, finding common ground, offering support on projects, or subtly introducing your ideas into conversations. Each of these steps is purposeful, contributing to your larger goal while simplifying your decisions.

Outlining the strategies you want to use is also important for creating a roadmap for your desired destination. Each strategy should align with your goals. This planning helps minimize your stress when making decisions in the moment because you've already considered the best course of action. This will also increase your ability to stay calm and composed, which is highly effective in dark manipulation.

Developing a strategist's mindset requires self-awareness, meticulous planning, and visualization techniques. Understanding and staying true to your core values ensures that your dark manipulation strategies are ethical and authentic. Define specific, measurable goals will keep you focused and accountable, while visualizing desired outcomes will enhance your confidence and connections to your goals. Finally, outlining your purposeful strategies gives you a roadmap, which simplifies your journey and reduces decision fatigue.

**Crafting a Step-by-Step Strategic Plan**

Crafting structured, actionable plans will significantly affect your personal and professional life. By breaking down larger goals into smaller, achievable steps, the process will feel less overwhelming, and you can keep track of your progress more efficiently. When facing a significant goal, it might feel stressed about its size; however, breaking it down into smaller, bite-sized tasks changes a mountain into manageable hills.

Imagine aiming to improve your networking skills to advance your career. Instead of deciding to "network more," start by breaking down this goal into more specific actions. For example, attending one networking event per month, setting up two coffee meetings per week, and following up on LinkedIn connections within 48 hours. Each action is targeted and measurable, making it easier to track your progress and keeps you motivated. This method helps simplify the overall objective while providing you with clarity on what needs to be done next.

*Setting Timelines*

Creating clear timelines is another important aspect of your structured plan. Timelines can give you a sense of urgency and ensure you don't procrastinate. They serve as checkpoints for assessing your progress, helping you maintain your accountability throughout the process. For example, if you're working towards becoming a more assertive communicator, then set specific deadlines for completing related tasks. Decide to read a book on assertiveness by the end of the month or attend a workshop within the next quarter. Each timeline will ensure that you stay on track with your goals.

## Clarify Resources

Having steps and timelines in place isn't enough; identify the necessary resources and build a support network. Resources include books and courses, mentors, and peer groups, who can give you guidance and encouragement. A support system is important because it gives you emotional backing and practical advice. If you're working on improving your public speaking skills, then join a Toastmasters group and engage with like-minded people who have similar goals to help boost your motivation and resilience.

Think about a scenario in your personal relationships where you'd like to manage conflicts more effectively. Identify resources like conflict resolution workshops, self-help books, or online courses. Simultaneously, building a support system involves friends and family who understand your goals and can provide constructive feedback. Having access to the right tools and a network of supportive people enhances your ability to execute your strategies.

## Evaluating Obstacles

Preparing for challenges before they happen enables you to create proactive solutions and helps you maintain a positive outlook when difficulties happen. Obstacles are unavoidable, but when you anticipate them, it gives you the opportunity to minimize their impact. Say you aim to become more influential at work. Potential obstacles might include resistance from colleagues, lack of confidence, or limited opportunities to showcase your leadership skills. Identifying these hurdles early on, your strategies can help you find ways to overcome them, like seeking mentorships, practicing public speaking, or volunteering for leadership roles in team projects.

## Think Ahead

Thinking ahead and considering what might go wrong prevents the opportunity to get caught off guard and enables you to tackle issues head-on. Let's revisit the goal of enhancing your communication skills. Possible obstacles involve time constraints, fear of public speaking, or lack of immediate feedback. To prevent this, choose a specific time for practice, manage your anxiety, and seek environments where constructive feedback is available, like practice sessions with trusted friends and colleagues. Knowing what hinders your progress allows you to create contingency plans, ensuring you stay on track with your goals even when faced with setbacks.

Creating structured, actionable plans involves several key steps: breaking down larger goals, setting timelines, identifying resources, building supportive networks, and evaluating potential obstacles. These components play an important role in ensuring your plan is successful and holds its momentum.

Breaking your process down will make your goals seem less daunting and give you a clear roadmap to follow. Setting timelines for each step gives you a sense of urgency and accountability, keeping you on track. Identifying resources and establishing a support network gives you the tools and encouragement to navigate your journey. Lastly, evaluating potential obstacles prepares you to face challenges proactively, building resilience and a positive outlook.

## Adapting to Changing Circumstances and Feedback

We live in a fast-paced and ever-changing world. Having a resilient and flexible mindset is crucial when aiming to navigate these dynamics effectively using dark manipulation tactics. Flexibility is not just about being able to bend without breaking; it's about changing your strategies in real-time, adapting to changing dynamics, and remaining strategic while under pressure.

Imagine working on a project with a deadline. You get new information that changes everything, and your plan is no longer viable. What do you do? If you're flexible, you won't panic. Instead, you reassess the situation, gather new data, and adjust your strategy. The ability to change allows you to stay on track with your goals, maintaining your composure and strategic edge even when things don't go as planned.

*Feedback*

Accepting and analyzing feedback is a valuable tool for personal growth. Getting constructive feedback might sting initially, but instead of taking it personally, see it as an opportunity to sharpen your skills. Feedback will help you see the blind spots in your personality and show you where you should improve. It creates a growth mindset, where you can see every piece of feedback as a stepping stone towards becoming a better version of yourself. Whether it's feedback from your boss, a friend, or someone else, embrace it, dissect it, and use it to hone your skills.

*Adjusting Your Strategies*

Adjusting your strategies based on your observations is an important element in developing a strategist's mindset. This demonstrates your competency and emotional intelligence. Let's say you've been observing the behavior of your team during meetings. You might see certain approaches leading to engagement while others do not. This information can help you adjust your strategy to create a more productive and engaging discussion. This adjustment will also show you're attuned to your environment and you're capable of making informed decisions to benefit everyone.

Proactivity means you're not waiting for things to go wrong before making changes. It's about anticipating potential issues and addressing them before they become bigger problems. For example, noticing a colleague struggling with their workload, offer assistance or suggest a more effective way to work to prevent burnout and improve productivity. This kind of foresight sets you apart as a leader who is both competent and emotionally intelligent.

*Continuous Learning*

Learning from interactions you have is important for long-term strategy development. Every conversation, meeting, or negotiation offers a wealth of lessons. Pay attention to what went as planned and what didn't. Reflect on these interactions and think about how you can use these lessons in the future. Continuous learning is about refining your strategies based on past experiences. Over time, this helps enhance your effectiveness and ensures you're always improving.

For example, let's say you conducted a presentation that didn't go as expected. Instead of thinking about the negative outcome, look for what went wrong. Was the audience distracted? Did you misjudge the level of detail needed? Use these insights to improve your next presentation. Each iteration makes you better and more confident in your skills.

Flexibility, getting feedback, proactive adjustments, and continuous learning are all interconnected elements that contribute to a resilient mindset. Together, these elements form the backbone of a strong strategist's mindset, enabling you to navigate the difficulties of your personal and professional relationships with confidence and assertiveness.

## Examples of Effective Dark Manipulation

Understanding how dark manipulation can be applied in real-life scenarios helps ground the theory in practical experience and provides solid examples to emulate and learn from.

### *Personal Relationships*

Start with considering personal relationships. Analyzing successful dark manipulation within these contexts shows how transformative this tactic is. For example, think about influencing your partner's decisions to align more with a shared goal or mutually beneficial goal without overt pressure. This includes framing discussions in a way that allows your partner to feel like the final decision-maker or planting ideas that seem original to them. Evaluating these strategies brings a positive change in your relationships and demonstrates their applicability and effectiveness. These instances give you clear evidence of how dark manipulation maintains harmony and pushes joint objectives forward.

### *Professional Settings*

Consider your professional relationships. Keep ethical considerations and career growth benefits in mind when exploring dark manipulation in the workplace. For example, imagine a situation where an employee is skillfully navigating office politics to secure a promotion by associating themselves with an influential mentor and undermining their achievements or fostering alliances that position them as an invaluable part of the organization. Understanding the ethical boundaries here is important. Using dark manipulation to elevate your career while preserving integrity ensures long-term benefits without damaging reputations or relationships. Examining these contexts shows the strategic mastery needed for professional advancement and signifies the importance of maintaining ethical standards.

## *Examining Social Manipulations*

Your next step is to examine social manipulations to reveal key insights into interpersonal skills and unspoken group dynamics. For example, consider someone's skills in navigating social gatherings or community events. They use body language, tone modulation, and selective engagements to sway opinions their way and influence group decisions. This requires observing and understanding the power structures within the group and using subtle cures to position themselves as the right person and steer conversation in the direction of the desired outcome. Recognizing and practicing these skills encourages readers to hone their own capabilities in real-life situations, facilitating smoother interactions and more effective social movements. Understanding the undercurrents of group dynamics enhances your influence within any social context.

## *Investigating Modern Media*

Your final step is to investigate modern media examples to give yourself a look at how manipulation tactics are used in everyday life and society. Television shows, movies, and even the news can show characters or public figures who use manipulation to achieve your goals. These examples give you visuals that illustrate strategic thinking in action, making the concept more relatable and easier to grasp. Highlighting specific cases from popular media makes the discussions engaging and reinforces the societal relevance of these tactics.

Identifying and understanding these manipulative strategies in media can empower you to recognize similar patterns in your own life and use those insights to your advantage.

**Segue**

This chapter covered a lot of ground, including understanding your core values to visualize your desired outcome and outlining strategies. It's clear that having strong core values keeps you grounded, ensuring your actions are ethical and authentic. Setting specific, measurable goals helps you maintain focus, while visualization makes these goals easier to achieve. Break down larger goals into smaller steps, set timelines, and prepare for obstacles to simplify your journey and boost your confidence. Remember, adaptability is key. Stay open to feedback and ready to adjust when putting these strategies into practice. Observe what works for you and what doesn't to help you refine your approach so you can continue to get your desired outcome. Real-world examples of strategic manipulation, both personal and professional, give you valuable insights and practical application. Combining solid planning with flexibility and learning, you'll have all the tools needed to navigate complex responsibilities and achieve your goals effectively.

## Chapter 8
# HEALTHIER DYNAMICS IN PROFESSIONAL RELATIONSHIPS

Creating and maintaining healthier dynamics in your professional relationships is important when attempting to navigate your career with confidence and authority. Whether you're starting your working career or you want to elevate your career, understanding the intricacies of these interactions can make a world of difference. Developing solid professional relationships will open doors and foster an environment where you can thrive and succeed.

This chapter discusses various techniques to help you build and sustain healthy professional relationships. We'll look at how to establish your presence and authority at work, ensuring you resonate in your professional setting. Mastering your body language is another key aspect we'll be discussing, including insights on how non-verbal cues can enhance your interactions and perceptions among colleagues. We'll discuss the significance of clear and assertive verbal communication to articulate your ideas effectively. This chapter will equip you with practical tools and strategies to cultivate a positive and impactful presence in your professional life so you can use dark manipulation strategies effectively.

## Establishing Your Presence and Authority at Work

Establishing your authority within your workplace requires that you create your own personal brand. This is the way you present yourself to the world, emphasizing what makes you valuable in your position. This doesn't mean you need to reinvent yourself; instead, it requires highlighting your strengths and qualities that align with your career goals. Your personal brand should show how competent you are within your professional setting, making it easier to recognize and respect your abilities.

### *Identify Your Core Values and Skills*

Building your personal brand requires finding your core values and skills. Ask yourself what you're passionate about and what unique skills you can present to the company. Then, communicate these elements consistently across your professional portfolio, including your resume, LinkedIn profile, and even the interactions you have at work daily. Consistency is key when building your brand because it'll help people remember you and associate you with specific qualities and achievements. For example, if you want to be known for your problem-solving skills, share your stories and examples of where you successfully tackled challenging situations and made a difference.

Once your brand is created, it's time to maintain it, which requires continuous effort. Stay updated in your field, engage in relevant conversations, and show your accomplishments. Networking events, professional groups, and social media platforms are excellent places where you can keep your brand alive. Remember, a strong personal brand will enhance your visibility and position you as a go-to expert within your industry.

## *Mastering Body Language*

Mastering your body language is yet another powerful tool in your arsenal. Non-verbal cues can have a significant impact on how others see you. Simple gestures like maintaining eye contact and good posture can show a lot about your confidence level and leadership skills. Eye contact shows you're engaged and honest, while good posture shows your readiness and control. Stand tall, shoulders back, and meet people's gaze confidently during conversations and presentations.

Mind your facial expressions and hand movements. A genuine smile can make you more approachable, whereas frowning or crossing your arms might come off as being defensive or uninterested. Use open gestures to show you're receptive and actively listening. For example, nodding occasionally while someone speaks indicates you're engaged and valuing their input. These adjustments in body language help you build rapport and establish yourself as someone confident and thoughtful.

## *Verbal Language*

Verbal communication requires articulating your ideas clearly and confidently. Clear communication goes beyond speaking loudly or slowly; it's about being precise and concise with your words. When presenting an idea, start with your main point first before diving into details. This structure helps your audience follow along and understand your message better.

Using assertive language during your communications with other people helps you get your ideas through clearly. This includes using phrases like "I believe," "I recommend," or "My suggestion is," which reinforces the fact that you have considered your idea thoroughly before. Avoid ambiguity that undermines your authority. Be prepared to support your ideas with data and examples. This demonstrates that your recommendations are grounded in research and experience, making it easier for colleagues to trust and follow your lead.

## *Leveraging Feedback*

Leveraging feedback is essential for professional growth. Asking for feedback is not weak but rather a willingness to continuously improve. Ask for constructive criticism from peers, mentors, and supervisors to help you find areas where you can enhance your performance. This proactive behavior shows you're committed to developing your skills and taking your responsibilities seriously.

When someone offers feedback, listen without interrupting and consider the suggestions they give. It's natural to want to become defensive, but you need to stay open-minded to benefit from the insights given. Afterwards, reflect on the feedback and create a plan to implement any changes. Whether it's improving your presentation skills, learning new software, or managing your time, acting on the feedback shows that you want to improve yourself.

Remember, you need to give feedback too. Doing this thoughtfully can strengthen your relationships and create a culture of mutual respect. Approach feedback discussing with the intention to help, focusing on behaviors and outcomes instead of personal attributes. Be specific about what worked and what the other person can improve and give them clear examples. Constructive feedback contributes to better team dynamics and enforces a supportive workplace.

## **Negotiation Tactics to Achieve Desired Results**

Understanding various negotiation tactics to help you get what you want is important if you want to be successful with your dark manipulation strategies. This section discusses various tactics you need to be aware of.

## *Preparation and Research*

Effective negotiations start with preparation and doing your research. Think about it like studying for an important exam. The more you know, the better you will do. Understand the specifics of what you want to achieve with your negotiations and get all the information together about the person you are negotiating with to put you in a better position. You'll be able to anticipate their needs and concerns; making it easier to find common ground to get your desired outcome.

For example, before you sit down to negotiate a raise with your boss, research industry standards for the role you're in as well as the region. Knowing your worth and being ready with data will support your request. This makes you more prepared and signals competence and professionalism. Being informed will give you the ability to counter any arguments that may come up and pivot as needed without losing sight of your goals.

### *Using Assertive Language*

After preparing yourself, it's time to focus on how you will communicate. Using assertive language when negotiating can affect the outcome. Assertiveness involves being clear, direct, and respectful without sounding aggressive or submissive. It'll help you express your needs and desires confidently while showing that you respect the perspective of the other person.

Start with something like "I'd like to discuss the possibility of a raise based on my performance and market standards," instead of saying, "I was hoping we could discuss my salary." This shift in how you address the issue will show your confidence and clarity, eliminating vagueness and indecisiveness. Practicing assertive communication can make a big difference in how you are seen, giving you better outcomes.

### *Finding Win-Win Scenarios*

It's important to create win-win scenarios when negotiating. It's about getting what you want, understanding the goals and needs of the other party, and working towards solutions that benefit you both. This approach helps you create and maintain a positive professional relationship and encourages future collaboration.

Think about negotiating a project with a colleague that has a timeline. Instead of insisting on a deadline, ask questions to understand their constraints and pressures. This helps you find a middle ground to satisfy both parties. For example, instead of setting unrealistic deadlines, propose phased deliveries where both immediate and long-term goals are met.

Mutual benefits will create goodwill, making the other party more willing to work with you. Furthermore, show that you care about their needs as much as your own, so they are encouraged to negotiate in good faith, which increases the chances of reaching a satisfactory agreement for both parties.

## *Handling Objections Gracefully*

Finally, you need to handle objections during negotiations with grace. Handling objections gracefully is essential for keeping the conversation productive and respectful. Objections aren't necessarily deal-breakers; they can be opportunities to further clarify and compromise on your negotiation.

When you come across an objection, listen and understand where the other person is coming from. Instead of defending your position aggressively, take a moment to consider their point of view. Receptiveness to objections can lead to more innovative solutions that no-one has considered initially.

For example, if your boss raises the concern of not having a budget to pay your raise, then don't dismiss them. Instead, acknowledge it and suggest an alternative, like phased increases or additional performance-based bonuses. This shows you're willing to collaborate with them and find creative solutions to your problems, which can be very appealing.

## **Building Alliances and Networks Strategically**

Networking and building alliances are important for professional growth and influence, especially for women aiming to navigate their careers with confidence and authority. This opens doors for new opportunities, creates a support system, and enhances your credibility within your chosen field.

## *Identify Key Stakeholders*

This is an important step in networking effectively. Key stakeholders include individuals who hold significant influence within an organization or industry. Finding these people is important because they can give you visibility and open doors for you to new opportunities. To identify these stakeholders, start by analyzing your workplace or industry landscape. Who are the decision-makers? Who has the power to influence the outcomes you desire? After acknowledging these individuals, it's time to make an effort to understand their roles, interests, and how your goals align with theirs. For example, if you're working in a tech company, contact the head of product development as a key stakeholder for you. Building rapport with these people leads to collaborative projects that showcase your skills and enhance your profile within the company.

Building a relationship with these individuals involves more than just knowing who they are; it's about building connections. This requires regular communication and a willingness to give them support when needed. Sending occasional emails sharing interesting articles, invitations to events, or checking in on them can go a long way. It's equally important to strike a balance—too much communication can be pestering, whereas too little may lead to being forgotten. Think of relationship-building as tending to your garden; it requires patience, consistency, and care. Over time, these efforts results in stronger professional ties.

## *Networking Events*

Networking events are excellent places to meet influential people and increase your credibility. These events give you unique opportunities to interact with industry leaders, potential mentors, and peers who can be valuable contacts. Making the most of these events requires research beforehand. Knowing who'll be attending, planning who you want to connect with, and preparing talking points relevant to your outcome is essential. Include an elevator pitch about your career aspirations and your current projects, and don't shy away from introducing yourself to people at the end of the event. This includes a short email thanking them for their time and mentioning something about the discussion you had, which will leave a lasting impression.

Attending these events helps boost your visibility within your professional circle, signalling you're committed to your career growth. For example, Emily, a young woman in finance, always attended industry conferences and actively participated in panel discussions. This helped her learn from experts and positioned her as a knowledgeable and engaged professional, leading to numerous speaking invitations and job offers.

### *Follow-Up and Maintain*

Following up and maintaining the connections you build is perhaps one of the most important aspects of networking. Not following up may not leave a lasting impression. When meeting someone at a networking event or elsewhere, make a note to send a follow-up message within a few days. Share updates, congratulate them on their achievements, or invite them to other events. This effort reinforces your presence and demonstrates your commitment to building a strong professional relationship with them.

You should maintain these connections without coming across as reliant or insincere. Consider Sarah, who met a potential mentor at a conference. She followed up with a thoughtful email and periodically sent updates on her career progress. She also offered her help whenever possible, creating a balance and mutually beneficial relationship that lasted for years.

### **Handling Competition and Politics Effectively**

Navigating competitiveness and corporate politics is an important skill for fostering healthier professional relationships. This section will explore how you can handle these dynamics to enhance your workplace experience.

## *Understanding Workplace Dynamics*

It's important to analyze the competitive landscape and general environment within your workplace. Every company has its own unique culture, norms, and unspoken rules that influence how people interact and compete. Familiarize yourself with these elements to help you navigate them effectively. Observe how colleagues communicate, how decisions are made, and who holds the most informal power. This knowledge gives you an advantage in understanding the undercurrents that drive behaviors in your organization.

Once you understand workplace dynamics, it's time to develop strong personal strategies. This involves crafting a personalized approach to competition and self-assertion without stepping on other people. Reflect on your strengths, weaknesses, and career goals. You can use your unique skills to stand out by using professional boundaries. It's important to assert yourself confidently while being respectful of those around you. For example, if you're in a meeting and someone interrupts you, calmly reclaim your space by saying, "I appreciate your input, but let me finish my point." This will show confidence and maintain respect.

Understanding power dynamics is just as important. This is about hierarchy and the flow of information and resources. Who controls what information? Who makes the final decisions? Understanding these aspects lets you position yourself strategically. For example, if you know a particular manager values innovation, then tailor your project proposals to highlight creative solutions. This helps you align your values and increases your chances of gaining their support.

## *Engaging in Competition*

Instead of looking at competition as a threat, see it as an opportunity for growth and team enhancement. Participating in constructive competition means you'll push yourself to excel while encouraging your peers to do the same. For example, if a colleague excels in a particular area, take it as motivation to improve your own skills instead of feeling envious. This mindset helps you create a more supportive environment where everyone is motivated to bring their best selves to work.

Mentorship programs or peer reviews can also be great ways to channel competition positively. Share knowledge and provide feedback to help others grow and refine your own understanding and skills.

*Building Rapport*

This goes beyond just knowing people; it's about building trust and mutual respect. Engage in conversations, show interest in colleagues' projects, and offer support where possible. Building rapport requires consistency and reliability. Setting a deadline means that you will ensure that you meet it. These actions speak volumes and build professional credibility.

A practical guideline to remember is maintaining a balance between asserting yourself and collaborating with others. Balancing these aspects helps you create a harmonious yet competitive environment. For example, when presenting a new idea, be assertive about its benefits and invite feedback from your team. This will show your leadership skills while valuing your collective input.

Another important guideline is regularly revisiting and reflecting on your strategies. The corporate landscape is ever-changing, and what works now might not work tomorrow. Set time aside to evaluate your approach to competition and office politics. Are you still serving your goals? Are there any adjustments needed based on recent changes in the workplace? Adapting ensures that your strategies stay relevant and effective.

Remember to maintain healthy professional relationships. It requires continuous effort, self-awareness, and adaptability. Celebrate your success and learn from setbacks. Every experience is an opportunity to refine your skills and strategies, making you more knowledgeable about navigating the intricate dynamics of the workplace.

**Segue**

This chapter discussed various techniques for building and maintaining healthy relationships. From creating a personal brand that highlights your strengths to mastering your body language and clear communication, these strategies empower you to navigate your career with confidence. We've explored how consistency, assertiveness, and active listening can cement your authority and foster a positive working environment. We also discussed how you can leverage feedback and understand the nuances of competition and office politics. By establishing genuine connections with the help of strategic networking and creating a supportive rapport with key stakeholders, you'll be better equipped to handle workplace dynamics effectively. Remember, the goal is to stand out and create mutual respect and understanding, creating a more inclusive and dynamic professional landscape.

## Chapter 9

# TRANSFORMING INTO A FEMME FATALE

Transforming yourself into a femme fatale is about embracing the traits that make you captivating and influential through dark manipulation strategies. This chapter delves into using confidence, mystery, and charm to create an irresistible persona. Confidence helps you stand out and commands respect in any setting. It's about believing in yourself and projecting self-assurance. When you're confident, your body language will show authority, making people take notice of you. Imagine walking into a room knowing all eyes are on you because of the way you present yourself. You will discover how you can add a touch of mystery to keep people intrigued and eager to know more. A femme fatale doesn't reveal everything immediately; she holds back enough to maintain an air of enigma. This chapter will help you use your charm to make every interaction memorable.

### Traits of a Femme Fatale: Confidence, Mystery, and Charm

A femme fatale has various traits that make them attractive to the people they come across. Additionally, these traits help you elevate your dark manipulation strategies so you can get your desired outcomes faster and more efficiently. This section discusses each of these traits to start using them effectively.

## *Confidence*

This is possibly one of the most important traits of being a femme fatale. The self-assurance that comes with confidence demands attention and respect, creating a foundation for how you are perceived by others. Confidence allows you to step into any room with an undeniable presence. Confidence is about believing in yourself while projecting it outward. Confidence makes you stand taller, make better eye contact, and speak more clearly. The way you carry yourself can help captivate those around you.

For example, think about the times when you observed someone who shows confidence. They might not seek validation from others because their aura speaks for itself. This is the kind of assurance that's magnetic. In professional settings, this trait can lead to better opportunities as your colleagues and management notice you during various situations. In personal relationships, it helps you establish boundaries and ensures mutual respect.

## *Mystery*

Mystery is about intrigue. A femme fatale knows the value of being enigmatic. You don't reveal everything about yourself immediately; instead, you choose to reveal bits and pieces of yourself gradually. This keeps people guessing and coming back, wanting to know more. This is powerful because it creates ongoing curiosity and excitement.

Look at a few classic film characters like Gilda or Jessica Rabbit, who left a lot to the imagination, yet it was intriguing to watch. Keeping certain aspects of their personality shrouded in mystery, they were able to maintain their irresistible charm. In real time, maintaining a bit of secrecy about your thoughts, feelings, and past experiences can work the same way. It's not about being dishonest; instead, it's about being selective about what you're willing to share with others. This selectivity can add layers to your persona, making every interaction a deeper experience.

## *Charm*

Charm (as mentioned previously) is a defining characteristic that boosts your influence to another level. Your charm can be seen as a magical ability to make others feel good in your presence. It requires that you show warmth, wit, and authenticity. This does not mean you put on an act; instead, it's about finding new ways to connect with others. This might involve showing interest in the lives of others, sharing a laugh, or offering thoughtful compliments.

A charming woman can effortlessly engage with others in conversation, often leaving them feeling valued and appreciated. An example is someone who remembers even the smallest details about others and brings them up in future conversations, showing that she listened and cares about the other person. This simple act can help you build stronger connections with others and leave lasting impressions. In both personal and professional settings, charm can make your interactions smoother and more enjoyable, paving the way for better relationships and collaborations.

Incorporating these traits into your daily life can help you transform into a formidable force. A femme fatale isn't merely a collection of characteristics; she's the harmonious blend of these elements. All of them complement each other, which creates a balanced and captivating persona. Confidence helps you lay the foundation, where mystery builds a layer of allure and charm solidifies connections.

For example, imagine a woman stepping into a social gathering. Her confident posture grabs the attention right away. As she interacts, her enigmatic answers to questions pique interest, while her charismatic way of engaging with people makes the entire experience memorable for everyone she connects with. This integrated approach ensures that she stands out in the crowd.

Remember that incorporating these traits doesn't require drastic changes. You can start by practicing minor acts of confidence, like voicing your opinions in meetings, standing tall when you talk, and making eye contact when talking to someone. Adding mystery might require that you become more mindful about what you share. Embrace the idea that it's okay to keep some things to yourself, letting only trusted individuals see various sides of you. When it comes to charm, you need to focus on building genuine connections. Show interest in the stories others share, share laughter, and bring positive energy to your interactions.

## Incorporating Intrigue Into Your Persona

A femme fatale is not just a cliche from various film characters; she embodies a dynamic and alluring personality that captivates and commands attention. Creating this aura involves more than just external allure. It requires that you add layers of intrigue to your personality. This section will dive into various techniques to help you enrich your interactions, making you more engaging and impactful.

### *Personal Stories*

Sharing your personal stories can be an excellent starting point for creating this complexity. Imagine meeting someone who shares the same facts as everyone else; it becomes forgettable. But when you incorporate your personal experiences into your storytelling, you can create a compelling narrative. For example, instead of saying you enjoy hiking, talk about a solo hike you went on where you found something profound about yourself or the nature around you. By doing this, you will add depth and uniqueness to your story, which will help keep people interested in what you have to say next. Selective storytelling isn't about deceit; it's about highlighting the parts of your life that showcase your most intriguing qualities.

### *Selective Sharing*

The next important point is selective sharing, which is an important art to master. Not everyone needs to know everything about you. This tool can be powerful in social dynamics. Think about classic femme fatales in literature and film; they were never open books. Holding back certain details will help keep others curious about you and invested in learning more. For example, if you are asked about your plans for the weekend, then you can give a hint or tease the person asking instead of giving them a full disclosure: "I have something exciting lined up, but let's see how it goes." This will make everyday conversations more engaging by nurturing curiosity and anticipation.

## *Non-Verbal Communication*

The facial expressions and body language you use are another important aspect of elevating your allure without saying a word. A slight smile, a raised eyebrow, or a poised posture can show confidence and enigma. Non-verbal cues often speak louder than words, and it can leave a lasting impression. Maintaining eye contact, for example, shows interest and confidence, while a well-timed glance can show contemplation or a hidden depth of thought. Everyone has unique features and ways of expressing themselves, so it's essential to find what works best for you and practice these subtle forms of communication.

## *Engaging Conversations*

This is yet another fundamental aspect to add layers of intrigue to your interaction style. It's not enough to talk about yourself; knowing how to ask the right questions and listening actively can make dialogues more captivating. When communicating with others, steer away from discussion about topics that reveal insights into the other person's life and thoughts instead of asking surface-level questions like "What do you do for work?" Consider more thought-provoking questions like "What inspired you to choose your career path?" This will elevate the conversation and position you as a thoughtful and engaging conversationalist.

## *Balance Openness*

This gives another element of enigma that provides a strategic advantage in your social dynamics. Sharing just enough to be relatable while keeping others intrigued and wanting to learn more. An effective way to implement this is through controlled vulnerability. You can show glimpses of your passions, fears, or dreams, but not all at once. For example, if discussing a project you're passionate about, express your excitement and dedication, but you need to leave room for more detailed discussions later. This will give you the opportunity to build a layered image over time, ensuring repeated engagement and interest.

To bring these techniques together, self-awareness and reflection are important. Take time to reflect on your interactions and responses. What worked? What didn't? How did people react? Adjustments based on these reflections can help refine your approach, ensuring that each encounter is a learning experience for crafting a more intriguing persona.

You need to practice and put in a deliberative effort to start incorporating these strategies into your daily life. Over time, they will become more natural to you and your personality, enhancing your ability to captivate and influence the people around you. Embrace the journey of transforming yourself into a femme fatale by focusing on your personal storytelling, selective sharing, non-verbal cues, and engaging conversations. This will give you a multi-faceted, intriguing presence that leaves a memorable impact on everyone you meet.

## Using Allure to Captivate and Influence

In order to understand how to use your personal allure as a tool to influence others while ensuring that you maintain ethical boundaries, it's important to understand what makes you allure. Allure is a combination of confidence, mystery, and charisma that draws people in. By possessing these traits, you can effectively leverage charm to navigate social and professional relationships.

### *Understanding Allure*

Allure is more than just physical appearances; it has a unique blend of personality traits, behaviors, and attributes. Confidence plays a significant role here. When you believe in yourself, others will follow shortly after. Being authentic and true to yourself makes you more magnetic. People are naturally drawn to people who exhibit self-assurance and authenticity in their personalities.

The mystery you show will add another layer of allure. This means not revealing every detail about yourself. Balance is key here, because too much mystery can make you come across as aloof, while too little can reduce your mystique.

Charisma is the emotional icing on your manipulation cake. It's about connecting with people on an emotional level, making them feel valued and heard. This could be a warm smile, thoughtful question, and listening actively, which can all make you irresistible. Understanding these components allows you to leverage your personal allure effectively.

## *Awareness of Surroundings*

You can use your environment to enhance your allure and amplify your presence. The ambiance, setting, and time of day can all play a role in how others see you. For example, dim lighting can create a more intimate atmosphere, making your interactions more impactful.

Consider how you are engaging with others. In a professional setting, subtlety and professionalism can contribute to your allure. In social settings, you can be relaxed and sociable to become approachable. Think about how the environments can highlight your best qualities. Your choice of clothes, tone of voice, and body language should also match the setting to help enhance your allure.

Knowing when to speak and when to listen can make another big difference. In group settings, contributing thoughtfully instead of frequently wanting to interrupt or give your opinion can make a big difference. Pay attention to the reactions of others so you can adapt and maintain control over the interactions.

## *Empowering Others*

The most overlooked aspect of allure is its ability to enhance your dark manipulation tactics. While personal charm can be seen as self-serving, it can also uplift those around you. Making others feel important and appreciated can help you build strong, positive relationships.

You can do this by giving others genuine compliments. This means you need to recognize someone's efforts or skills to help boost their confidence and create a bond with mutual respect. Encouraging collaboration and valuing the input you get from others can also help you generate a sense of camaraderie and shared purpose.

By creating an environment where people feel valued and respected, you're enhancing your own allure while fostering a positive environment. This kind of mutual empowerment can translate into stronger professional networks and deeper personal connections.

*Tactful Influence*

Influencing others ethically and respectfully is important for maintaining trust and integrity. The goal is to use manipulation tactics to guide opinions and feelings through transparent and respectful means to get the outcome you desire. You need to show interest in what others have to say to create a dialogue instead of a monologue to make others feel heard and respected.

Leading by example is another example. This means demonstrating behaviors and attitudes you would like to inspire in others. If you want to promote a collaborative work style, then you need to exemplify collaboration in your actions. People are more likely to follow someone who practices what they preach.

Giving constructive feedback is just as important. Instead of criticizing, provide suggestions for improvement. This will promote growth and foster supportive environments.

Finally, transparency is needed. Be clear about your intentions and goals. When you have hidden agendas, you undermine trust, which can backfire in the long run. By being open about your motives, you ensure that your influence is ethical and earned.

## Maintaining Control and Desirability

### *Boundaries*

Establishing clear yet flexible boundaries is essential for sustaining your personal control and desirability in your relationships and social interactions. Boundaries that act as invisible barriers can define what you are comfortable with and what you aren't. They can help communicate your values and expectations to others, giving you the opportunity to maintain your sense of autonomy and respect.

For example, you might set a boundary regarding your time by not answering work emails after 7 p.m., ensuring that you have time to recharge after work. Similarly, emotional boundaries can include not engaging in conversations that make you uncomfortable or drain your energy. It's important to clearly communicate your boundaries to people around you. A simple, direct conversation can often prevent misunderstandings and affirm your stance.

However, it's important to remember that your boundaries should remain flexible enough to accommodate unforeseen circumstances. Life is often unpredictable, and fixed boundaries can lead to unnecessary conflicts. Flexibility is when you know you should break the rules you have set without putting your core values at risk. For example, when a close friend needs your support at an hour outside of your ability, then you can make an exception to show empathy, which will strengthen the relationship without undermining your overall boundary.

### *Self-Care*

Prioritizing your self-care is another important technique for staying desirable and maintaining your personal control. Self-care goes beyond occasional pampering; it involves regular practices that nurture your physical, emotional, and mental well-being. When you prioritize your self-care, you signal to yourself and others that you value and respect your needs, which in turn makes you more desirable and balanced.

Self-care can include regular exercise, a balanced diet, enough sleep, and mindfulness activities like meditation or journaling to enhance your well-being. Taking care of your appearance can also help boost your confidence. You don't need to conform to beauty standards; instead, embrace your unique style and become comfortable in your own skin to exude authenticity and allure. Emotional self-care, on the other hand, means setting aside time for hobbies, spending time with loved ones, and seeking professional help when you need it.

Self-care involves saying no to situations and people who drain the energy out of me. This might mean that you need to turn down a social event when you need rest or decline additional responsibilities at work that will overextend you. By prioritizing your well-being, you preserve your energy for the things that truly matter, making you more present and effective in your interactions.

## *Self-Improvement*

Lifelong learning and self-improvement strategies for continuous growth are more important strategies. The world is constantly evolving, and so should we. Lifelong learning can help you stay stimulated and adaptable, making you more interesting and confident. Whether it's learning a new skill, reading books on various topics, or taking courses, continuous growth can also help you stay relevant and adaptable.

Self-improvement is not just limited to academic knowledge. Emotional intelligence, communication skills, and resilience are other areas where you can continuously grow. For example, developing better listening skills can improve your personal and professional relationships. Building resilience helps you bounce back from setbacks and helps you maintain your composure and dignity in challenging times.

Self-improvement also requires regular self-reflection so you can understand your strengths and areas for growth. Journaling or discussing your experience with a mentor or coach can give you valuable insights. Remember, the goal of self-improvement isn't about perfection; it's about progress. Celebrate your milestones, big and small, and be patient with yourself as you evolve.

## *Decision-Making*

Making the right decisions is another cornerstone of sustaining personal control in relationships and social interactions. Every choice you make should align with your values and desired outcomes, or they can take you further away from them. Learning to make informed decisions requires clarity about your core values, priorities, and long-term goals.

Start by thinking about what truly matters to you. This can be honesty, ambition, or compassion. Once you have a clear understanding of your values, you can use them as your compass for the decisions you make. When you are faced with a choice, you can ask yourself whether it aligns with your values and brings you closer to your goals. For example, if family is a core value, then you can choose a job that allows you to have a work-life balance.

Making strategic decisions also involves assessing the risks and benefits that come with the decision. Not every decision you make will be successful, but when you weigh the potential outcomes, it can help you make informed choices. Sometimes, taking calculated risks can give you significant growth and opportunities. Conversely, understanding when to say no will protect you from making decisions that could compromise your values or well-being.

Learning from your past decisions and reflecting on the choices that led to positive outcomes can also help you in the future. What were the factors? How did you feel? Use these lessons to help you with future decisions. Strategic decision-making isn't always about grand choices; everyday decisions can help shape your life.

Incorporating the strategies mentioned above can help sustain your personal control and desirability in your relationships and social interactions. These techniques can empower you to navigate life with confidence, ensuring that you maintain power while being true to yourself.

**Segue**

This chapter explored how confidence, mystery, and charm can enrich your interactions while elevating your presence. Confidence helps you stand tall and commands respect, while a dash of mystery keeps others intrigued and wanting more. Charm can add a magical touch, making people feel appreciated and valued in your presence. By blending these traits, you can navigate both personal and professional relationships with grace and influence.

In practical terms, you can start integrating small acts of confidence into your daily life, like speaking up in meetings, maintaining good posture, and making eye contact. By selecting what you want to share will create an air of mystery, revealing parts of yourself gradually. Practice charm by genuinely connecting with others, showing interest in their stories, and spreading positive energy. These steps will help you build a well-rounded and captivating persona, empowering you to command respect and leaving a lasting impression wherever you go.

## Chapter 10
# SUSTAINING LONG-TERM SUCCESS AND INFLUENCE

**M**aintaining your long-term dark manipulation success and influence is all about continuous learning and adapting. As the world and its interpersonal dynamics evolve, you need to stay ahead by refining your skills and strategies. By embracing a mindset of ongoing learning and self-improvement, you can ensure that your techniques stay effective. This chapter will dive into how you can keep up with psychological insights and manipulation strategies, which form the backbone of lasting success. It's not just about knowing the latest tactics, but also understanding the deeper principles behind them to make the methods you use more precise and impactful.

This chapter will discuss various educational resources you can use, including books, articles, seminars, and online courses, to enhance your skills. You will learn how practical applications of this knowledge can be implemented into real-life scenarios to identify motivations and tailor your strategies. We will also discuss self-reflection and why it's important, seeking constructive feedback, and maintaining your growth mindset. These are all important elements to fine-tune your approach to dark manipulation while ensuring you get the outcomes you desire. By the end of this chapter, you will have actionable steps on how to balance your power dynamics, adapt to changing personal and professional landscapes, and sustain the influence you have over the long term.

## Continually Refining Your Skills and Strategies

Continuous learning and skill enhancement are the foundation of sustained long-term success and influence. In an ever-changing world where interpersonal dynamics evolve constantly, you need to stay updated on psychological insights and dark manipulation strategies. Engaging in ongoing education ensures that the techniques you are using stay effective. Let's dive into this section so you can learn how to achieve this.

### *Educational Resources*

There are various educational resources available, including books, articles, seminars, and online courses, that can be a valuable resource of information and tools to help you enhance your skills. These resources will give you theoretical knowledge and practical applications you can use in real-life scenarios. For example, understanding the latest findings in behavioral psychology can help you identify underlying motivations and tailor your strategies to be more effective. Furthermore, you can engage in up-to-date materials to help keep you informed about ethical boundaries, helping you ensure that your dark manipulation techniques lead to the outcome you desire.

### *Self-Reflection*

Practicing self-reflection is another important aspect of ensuring your success. This process requires evaluation of your past actions, successes, and failures. Reflecting on your experiences gives you the opportunity to identify patterns that worked and what didn't. For example, you can consider situations where your dark manipulation tactics were especially successful. What contributed to that success? What was your tone, timing, or the words you used? You can also analyze the failures to find insights into what went wrong. Did you overlook certain cues? Were your assumptions incorrect? Understanding these aspects will help you refine your approach so you can do better in future interactions.

## *Journaling*

This is another effective tool when practicing self-reflection. By documenting your thoughts and experiences, you are creating a record you can revisit and analyze. This will help you recognize patterns and track your progress over time. You will also be able to reflect on your growth, both in terms of your skills and knowledge, reinforcing a sense of accomplishment, which will motivate you to keep improving.

## *Seeking Feedback*

Getting feedback from people you trust is another important aspect of enhancing your dark manipulation techniques. Constructive criticism can give you a fresh perspective and highlight the areas you might not have considered. Find individuals who are familiar with your goals and can give you honest, objective feedback. Remember that you need to be open to suggestions and be willing to make the necessary adjustments when collecting feedback. For example, if a close friend or mentor tells you that you are being too aggressive with your approach, then you might want to consider how you can modify your tactics to appear more assertive instead of being confrontational.

You can also get feedback from professionals like coaches or therapists, who can give you specialized insights. These experts possess a deeper understanding of interpersonal dynamics, and they can help you refine your techniques. Their objective observations can help you hone your skills. Remember, the goal of seeking feedback is to improve, so you should embrace critiques as opportunities for growth.

## *Growth Mindset*

Adopting a growth mindset is important to continuously develop personally and relationally. Embrace challenges, be open to change, and view setbacks as learning opportunities. A growth mindset can also help you improve your resilience and adaptability, which are both crucial traits for navigating the complexities of long-term dark manipulation strategies. When you are faced with challenges, see them as an opportunity to develop new skills or refine the ones you already have.

For example, if a particular strategy is not giving you the results you want, then a growth mindset will encourage you to explore alternative approaches instead of just giving up. It involves an iterative process of testing, learning, and adjusting. This flexibility will help enhance your ability to influence effectively and ensure that your methods remain relevant as situations and circumstances change. A growth mindset will also help you create a positive attitude towards learning. Instead of getting overwhelmed by the need to continuously update your knowledge, you will start to see it as an exciting journey of discovery and improvement.

## Balancing Power Dynamics Sustainably

Maintaining power balances relationships is important for preventing manipulation from turning toxic or damaging. Understanding the power equilibrium is the first step towards achieving this balance. Power dynamics exist in every relationship, whether personal or professional. Recognizing and maintaining healthy and mutual power dynamics ensures neither party feels undervalued or overpowered.

It's important in any relationship to be aware of the balance of power. One-sided power can often lead to resentment, unhappiness, and ultimately, the deterioration of your relationships. Healthy power dynamics involve mutual respect, where both parties feel heard and valued. For example, in a work setting, you need to ensure that your voice is heard just as loudly during meetings so you can prevent the feeling of being overshadowed by your colleagues.

### *Be Clear About Your Boundaries*

Your boundaries are just as important here, which means that you need to discuss them openly in order to sustain this balance. Clear and honest conversations about what is acceptable in your relationship will help you set expectations and prevent misunderstandings from forming.

This also requires discussing how much time you need for yourself, the kind of behavior you find acceptable, and how you want to handle conflicts. For example, you can say that you need some time alone after work to recharge, and you won't be available to engage during this time.

Some of the things that are crucial for open communication include being clear and specific about your needs and expectations. This once again includes using "I" statements during conversations. This will also ensure that there is a mutual agreement and understanding of these boundaries through active listening and feedback.

## *Avoid Overreliance*

You need to avoid being over reliant on your dark manipulation strategies in order to maintain your ethical power in your relationships. While manipulation can be harmless in order to influence the outcomes you want, being over-dependent on these strategies can break down trust and authenticity. Your authenticity involves being true to yourself and what you stand for. It's about using your dark manipulation strategies as tools instead of crutches. When authentic interactions form the foundation of your relationships, it will nurture genuine connection and trust.

For example, instead of always using subtle tactics to get your partner to do something, just ask them directly. If you are still not getting them to do what you want, then you can move on to using manipulation. Balancing manipulation with authenticity means that you need to acknowledge when you should be transparent and straightforward. This approach builds trust and strengthens your relationships because your partner will know they can count on you to be genuine.

## *Recognizing Distortion*

Signs of distortion in your manipulation strategies should be recognized to ensure that your actions are not harming your relationships. These can start small and harmless, but they can snowball into behavior that can negatively impact the other person in the long run.

You need to be aware of the signs that your manipulation strategies are becoming harmful so you can address them early.

This could include feeling guilty about your actions, noticing an increase in tension or conflict in your relationships, or experiencing negative emotional responses from the other person. If you realize that your partner is avoiding you, they come unusually defensive, or they seem withdrawn, then it could be a signal that your strategies are becoming harmful. Regular self-reflection and seeking feedback from trusted friends or mentors can give you insights into whether your actions are crossing certain boundaries.

It's important to change your approach when you start recognizing these signs. This includes open dialogue with the other person to understand their perspective and adjusting your behavior accordingly. Apologize when you need to and commit to more transparent and respectful methods moving forward. Remember that dark manipulation is about getting what you want without coming across as being manipulative in any way.

## Adapting to Evolving Personal and Professional Landscapes

One of the most crucial aspects of maintaining your long-term success and influence through dark manipulation is by observing changes in your environment. The environments related to your personal and professional environments can be a constant flux of change. Life circumstances can change, new people can enter your life, and your existing dynamics can shift. Being attuned to these changes gives you the opportunity to adjust your strategies accordingly instead of sticking to your outdated approach religiously. You need to practice active listening and pay close attention to verbal and non-verbal cues when observing these shifts. Take note of your partners, colleagues, and superiors' reactions to various situations, and become aware of changes in their behavior and attitudes.

Understanding these evolving dynamics, you can evolve your manipulative strategies more effectively to fit the new context. This is where emotional intelligence comes into play. It gives you the ability to perceive, evaluate, and manage your own emotions as well as those of other people. By leveraging this skill, you can learn to read between the lines and get a deeper insight into what drives those around you. For example, if a colleague was open to collaboration before and suddenly becomes reticent, then your advanced emotional intelligence skills can help you recognize this change so you can find a way to re-establish rapport. Leveraging emotional intelligence involves not just understanding the emotions of others, but also being aware of your own feelings and how they influence your interactions. This will help you stay calm and composed under pressure and you will prevent unnecessary conflicts from arising.

## *Building a Flexible Strategic Plan*

This is another crucial aspect because even when you have a good roadmap, it's just as important to ensure that this roadmap isn't set in stone. Creating a flexible plan gives you room for adjustments based on new information and changing circumstances. Start by outlining your main objectives and adding contingency plans based on different scenarios. This can include multiple approaches to achieving the same goal or setting up smaller, intermediary targets you can adjust over time. Flexibility in your strategy allows you to turn unexpected challenges or opportunities, making it easier for you to maintain momentum towards your long-term goals.

One way to incorporate flexibility into your strategy is by regularly reviewing and updating it. This includes periodically assessing your progress and the effectiveness of your tactics. Ask yourself questions like, "What's working well?" and "What needs to change?" Doing this will make it easier for you to catch any potential issues early on and adjust them accordingly. It can also keep your plans relevant and aligned with the current context, ensuring that you're always operating at your best.

## *Embrace Technology*

You should also start embracing technology and social changes. Technology advances rapidly and staying updated with the developments can give you a significant advantage. Social media, for example, has changed the way we communicate and interact with others, giving us new platforms where we can influence and connect with others. Understanding how to use these tools effectively can greatly enhance your ability to manipulate dynamics in both personal and professional settings. For example, knowing how to craft persuasive messages on social media can help you get support for your projects and ideas.

Except for social media, other technological advancements like artificial intelligence, big data, and virtual really offer new avenues for influence. These technologies can give you valuable insights into human behavior, helping you refine your dark manipulation strategies even more. For example, big data analytics can help you understand broader trends and patterns, allowing you to anticipate shifts before they happen so you can adapt accordingly.

Embracing technological and social changes also includes becoming aware of societal shifts, like changing norms and values. Public perceptions of ethics, diversity, and inclusivity have evolved, and being sensitive to these changes can help you navigate your relationships more effectively. Staying informed about these shifts gives you the opportunity to adjust your behavior and communication so you can align them with contemporary expectations and standards. This will also help you avoid potential pitfalls and demonstrate adaptability and forward-thinking traits, which can help you increase your influence significantly.

## Lessons From Long-Term Success Stories

In the modern world, stories of resilient women who have used manipulation techniques to achieve the success you want can be both inspiring and instructional. In this section, we'll delve into a few case studies that will show you how these women have navigated their paths, analyze their strategies, draw actionable lessons from readers, and encourage you to create your own success narrative.

### Lisa

Lisa is a young professional in the corporate world who has faced numerous challenges early on in her career. She felt unnoticed and undervalued; her ideas were often unheard in meetings, mostly dominated by colleagues who are more assertive. Instead of giving up, Lisa adopted dark manipulation techniques to make her voice heard. She started looking at the power dynamics and identified key influencers within her team. She built genuine relationships with these influencers, aligning her goals with theirs and finding ways to support their initiatives. Gradually, her strategic alliances helped her gain recognition, and she leveraged this newfound influence to push her projects forward. By using dark manipulation strategies, Lisa was able to climb the corporate ladder and secure a leadership position where she could make real change.

### Maria

Maria is another compelling example. She is an entrepreneur who had to navigate the cutthroat landscape of the startup world. Maria understood the importance of perception and using dark manipulation strategies to shape how investors and clients saw her business. She strategically highlighted her company's unique value proposition and crafted narratives that resonated with her audience. She also maintained transparency and integrity, ensuring that her manipulation stays authentic and allowed her to build a loyal customer base and attract significant investment, leading her startup to exponential growth.

Analyzing the strategies used by these successful women shows several common elements. Firstly, they both worked on building strong relationships. They recognized that manipulation strategies rely on mutual trust and benefit rather than deceit and exploitation. By investing their time and effort into building meaningful connections, they created a network of support that amplified their manipulation techniques to align with changing circumstances. They stayed vigilant, assessed the impact of their actions, and adjusted their strategies accordingly. This adaptability ensured that their dark manipulation strategies were effective and sustainable over the long term.

Applying the important lessons from these case studies can give you the guidance you need to enhance your interpersonal communication and relationship strategies. One actionable lesson is the importance of self-awareness. Understanding that your strengths, weaknesses, and motivation allow you to manipulate situations to your advantage without compromising your values. For example, if you excel at public speaking but struggle to speak one-on-one, then you can use this strength in group settings while finding ways to improve your personal connections. Another important lesson is the power of empathy. By putting yourself in others' shoes, you can improve your understanding of their needs and desires, enabling you to tailor your manipulation techniques to resonate with them. This approach will give you positive outcomes and strengthen relationships.

Sharing your personal successes is equally important to inspiring others and reinforcing your own growth. When you document your journey, you not only create a record of your achievements, but you also reflect on the challenges you've overcome and the strategies that worked for you. Sharing your stories with others can provide motivation and insight, helping them navigate similar paths. As you articulate your experiences, focus on the moments when ethical manipulation techniques played an important role, as well as when you were required to use dark manipulation. Highlight how your actions positively impacted your relationships and advanced your goals. This reflection will reinforce your understanding of the principles discussed and empower you to continue applying them effectively.

Noting your personal successes is not just about celebrating victories; it's also an opportunity to learn from your setbacks. Embrace the lessons from your failures and use them as stepping stones for future successes. By sharing these experiences, you can contribute to a culture of openness and continuous improvement. Your story can become a beacon of hope and inspiration for others facing the same challenges, demonstrating that dark manipulation, when applied thoughtfully, can lead to lasting success and influence.

**Segue**

By embracing dark manipulation techniques and committing to continuous self-improvement, you can easily navigate your personal and professional relationships with greater confidence and effectiveness. This chapter has highlighted the importance of refining your skills, seeking feedback, and maintaining a growth mindset in order to adapt to ever-changing dynamics. Remember, these techniques can help increase the possibility of you getting the outcomes you need and mutual respect instead of using deceit or coercion to do that.

As you apply these strategies, always remember the evolving landscape around you. Being observant and adaptable gives you the ability to modify your approach when needed, ensuring that you stay relevant and effective with your strategies. Keep building genuine connections and balancing authenticity with your influence tactics. By doing this, you will achieve your goals and cultivate stronger, more resilient relationships that stand the test of time.

# Conclusion

As we come to the end of our journey, I want you to take a moment to reflect on everything you learned. Every chapter has been a step towards helping you unlock your inner alpha female. Every page was a stride towards becoming more confident and assertive in your life, both personally and professionally. It's essential to recognize that this journey doesn't have a final destination; it's an ongoing road of self-discovery and empowerment.

Think about where you started. Maybe you started with feeling uncertain, lacked confidence, or you might have struggled with asserting yourself. Now, take a look at the progress you have made with the help of this book. You gained insights into interpersonal communication, relationship strategies, and the dynamics of dark manipulation. You've learned how you can harness these skills as tools for deceit and a powerful means of influence. This is just the beginning. The confidence you have built and the skills you have learned are the foundation on which you can continue to grow.

Manipulation is often seen as being negative, but it's important to understand the positive potential it has when you use it correctly. Use it wisely and watch it transform your interactions. When you approach manipulation with wisdom and ethical intentions, it becomes a powerful tool for shaping outcomes in your favor while maintaining respect and integrity in your relationships.

As you continue on this journey, continue to cultivate your emotional intelligence. It will be your ability to understand and manage your own emotions and the emotions of others. It's a skill that underpins successful manipulation and leadership. As you grow your emotional intelligence, you'll notice an increase in your ability to connect with others on a more meaningful level. This deeper understanding will help enhance your strategic ability, making your manipulative techniques more effective.

You should also consider the significance of emotional intelligence in your daily interactions. By recognizing the emotions around you, you can easily navigate conversations and relationships with greater ease and impact. You will be better equipped to read people, understand their motivations, and respond in ways that align with your goals. The more you work on developing your emotional intelligence, the more you will become influential and steer situations towards the outcomes you desire.

Committing to lifelong learning is another important aspect of becoming an alpha female. The techniques and strategies you've learned in this book are not static; they can evolve with your changing circumstances and relationships. Just as you would perfect a craft, remember to revisit and refine your skills regularly. Look to your future with an open mind, ready to adapt your emotional and manipulative strategies as life unfolds.

Lifelong learning requires that you seek out new knowledge and experiences that challenge you and contribute to your growth. It means that you need to be willing to question your assumptions, learn from your mistakes, and always strive to improve. By committing to this mindset, you will become more resilient and adaptable, qualities that will help you in all areas of your life. Embrace opportunities for growth, whether through reading, attending workshops, seeking mentorship, or simply engaging in reflective practices.

You should also recognize the importance of balance. While assertiveness and confidence are vital, empathy and compassion are tools. Striking the right balance between strength and sensitivity will make you a more formidable force in any setting. Remember that true empowerment doesn't mean overpowering others; it means fostering mutual respect and understanding.

Building healthy, supportive relationships is just as important on this journey. You need to surround yourself with people who uplift and inspire you. Look for those who challenge you to be your best self and will give you honest feedback. These relationships will act as a valuable support system as you continue to grow and evolve. In turn, be a source of support and inspiration for others. Share your knowledge and experience and help those around you to create your own confidence and assertiveness.

Remember that self-care is just as important. This means taking care of your physical, mental, and emotional well-being to maintain your progress. Make time for activities that nourish and energize you. Whether that's doing exercise, meditation, creative pursuits, or spending time with your loved ones, you need to make self-care a non-negotiable part of your routine. By maintaining your well-being, you will ensure that you have the energy and resilience to face challenges and seize opportunities.

Finally, you need to celebrate your achievements. Acknowledge the hard work and dedication you have put in up to this point. Recognize the courage it takes to step out of your comfort zone and embrace new ways of thinking and behaving. Celebrate each victory, no matter how small, knowing that each of these is a testament to your growth and determination.

As you move forward, carry this sense of accomplishment with you. Let it fuel your continued pursuits of excellence and empowerment. Know that you have the right tools, knowledge, and resilience to overcome any challenges you might face. Your journey is yours alone, and no one can take that away from you or the confidence you have built.

Your journey to becoming an alpha female is a dynamic and ongoing journey of self-discovery and empowerment. Embrace the skills and insights you've learned and use them responsibly and ethically to influence and lead. Build your emotional intelligence, commit to lifelong learning, maintain balance, build supportive relationships, prioritize self-care, and celebrate your achievements. Doing this will help you unlock your fullest potential and live a life of confidence, assertiveness, and fulfillment.

*Thank you for reading! If you enjoyed this book, please take a moment to leave a quick star rating for this author, and don't forget to check out the full library of interesting topics available in this author's library of work.*

# References

*Balancing empathy and assertiveness in conflict resolution.* (n.d.). FasterCapital. https://fastercapital.com/topics/balancing-empathy-and-assertiveness-in-conflict-resolution.html

Becky. (2014, April 6). *Balancing empathy and assertiveness.* Mantis Counseling and Coaching LLC. https://mantiscounselingandcoaching.com/2014/04/06/balancing-empathy-and-assertiveness/

Cherry, K. (2023, December 31). *5 key components of emotional intelligence.* Verywell Mind. https://www.verywellmind.com/components-of-emotional-intelligence-2795438

Constant, G. A. (2024, March 9). *The alpha female definition.* Linkedin. https://www.linkedin.com/pulse/alpha-female-dr-gene-constant-niqec

Dalla-Camina, M. (2023, April 2). *Reflections on feminine power.* Psychology Today. https://www.psychologytoday.com/ca/blog/real-women/202303/reflections-on-feminine-power

Dawson, S. (n.d.). *Harriet Tubman.* National Women's History Museum; National Women's History Museum. https://www.womenshistory.org/education-resources/biographies/harriet-tubman

Dickey, C. (2024, June 18). *Building strong interpersonal skills effective communication and boundaries.* Coachingly.

https://www.coachingly.ai/blog/single/building-strong-interpersonal-skills-effective-communication-and-boundaries

Dr Astray. (2020, March 19). *Communication tool: Assertive confrontation and boundary setting with the DESO script.* Dr. Astray. https://www.tatianaastray.com/managing-relationships/2020/3/18/communication-tool-assertive-confrontation-and-boundary-setting-with-the-deso-script

Duckworth, A. L., Gendler, T. S., & Gross, J. J. (2016). Situational strategies for self-control. *Perspectives on Psychological Science, 11*(1), 35–55. https://doi.org/10.1177/1745691615623247

Editor. (2023, September 3). *Boundary setting in communication: 5 ways to say no with respect.* Rcademy. https://rcademy.com/boundary-setting-in-communication/

Editors desk. (2024). *The intersection of personal branding and gender dynamics in the modern workplace.* No Worker Left Behind. https://noworkerleftbehind.org/the-intersection-of-personal-branding-and-gender-dynamics-in-the-modern-workplace/

*Effective communication instructor guide.* (2014). https://training.fema.gov/emiweb/is/is242b/instructor%20guide/ig_complete.pdf

*Effective communication skills.* (2024, March 4). Better Relationships. https://www.betterrelationships.org.au/effective-communication-skills/

*Elevate Your EQ: Emotional Intelligence Training for Personal Growth.* (n.d.). Kutskoconsulting. https://www.kutskoconsulting.com/blog/emotional-intelligence-training

*Empath.* (2023, June 21). Wikipedia. https://en.wikipedia.org/wiki/Empath

Espinosa, F. (2024, May). *Embracing vulnerability: My journey of personal growth and emotional intelligence.* Linkedin.

https://www.linkedin.com/pulse/embracing-vulnerability-my-journey-personal-growth-fernando-kixsc

Femme academy. (2023, August 2). *How to achieve the femme fatale mindset.* Lemon8-App. https://www.lemon8-app.com/femmefataleschool/7262712637962600965?region=us

Flamiano, M. (2024, September 4). *How to be a femme fatale (with pictures).* WikiHow. https://www.wikihow.com/Be-a-Femme-Fatale

Galsanjigmed, E., & Sekiguchi, T. (2023). Challenges women experience in leadership careers: An integrative review. *Merits, 3*(2), 366–389. MDPI. https://doi.org/10.3390/merits3020021

Gardenswartz Ph.D, C. (2024, July 30). *The art of listening: Improve communication with your partner.* Psychology Today. https://www.psychologytoday.com/ca/blog/the-discomfort-zone/202407/the-art-of-listening-improve-communication-with-your-partner

Grant, K. W. (2024, June 8). *Understanding and combatting psychological manipulation.* KevinGrant. https://www.kevinwgrant.com/blog/item/understanding-and-combatting-psychological-manipulation

Hakim, M. (2023, August 6). *Building emotional intelligence: Nurturing self-awareness and empathy.* Malaka Therapy. https://mhtherapy.ca/building-emotional-intelligence-nurturing-self-awareness-and-empathy/

Hoffman, M. (2023, November 13). *Empowering women in the workplace: 5 negotiation strategies for career advancement.* Vaco | Talent Solutions. https://www.vaco.com/blog/empowering-women-5-workplace-negotiation-strategies/

Holder, E. (n.d.). *Communication skills: 10 tips for effective communication.* Jostle. https://blog.jostle.me/blog/communication-skills

Hughson, C. (2020, September 16). *Communicate effectively by using active listening techniques.* Ivey Business School. https://www.ivey.uwo.ca/academy/insights/2020/09/communicate-effectively-by-using-active-listening-techniques/

Jansen, E. (2023, December 29). *Elevating emotional intelligence: Coaching strategies that work.* Quenza. https://quenza.com/blog/knowledge-base/coaching-emotional-intelligence/

Jiang, R. (2024, February 28). *Women leadership how can leverage feminine power.* Linkedin. https://www.linkedin.com/pulse/women-leadership-how-can-leverage-feminine-power-life-ran-jiang-3pptc

Leong, B. (2024, March 5). *Femininity in the workplace: Embracing strength and redefining power.* Linkedin. https://www.linkedin.com/pulse/femininity-workplace-embracing-strength-redefining-power-bianca-leong-khdfc

Leonnova. (2023, December 20). *Empower Growth with Emotional Intelligence.* Leonnova. https://leonnova.com/harnessing-emotional-intelligence/

Lopes, S. (2023, September 18). *Negotiate like a woman! On gender and negotiation working as a working woman.* The Corporate Sister. https://www.thecorporatesister.com/blog/negotiate-like-a-woman-on-gender-and-negotiation-working-as-a-working-woman/

Lau, J. (2023, November 21). *How Jacinda Ardern tackled public health crises in New Zealand.* News; Harvard T.H.Chan. https://www.hsph.harvard.edu/news/features/how-jacinda-ardern-tackled-public-health-crises-in-new-zealand/

*Manipulation: Mastering manipulation: Lady macbeth's strategic approach.* (2024, June 23). FasterCapital. https://fastercapital.com/content/Manipulation--Mastering-Manipulation--Lady-Macbeth-s-Strategic-Approach.html

McLeod, S. (2018). Maslow's Hierarchy of Needs. In *Canada College* (pp. 1–16). Simply Psychology. https://canadacollege.edu/dreamers/docs/Maslows-Hierarchy-of-Needs.pdf

McLeod, S. (n.d.). *Maslow's hierarchy of needs*. SimplyPsychology. https://www.simplypsychology.org/maslow.html

Moncrief, D. (n.d.). *ScholarWorks leadership influences of the veteran alpha female leader*. https://scholarworks.waldenu.edu/cgi/viewcontent.cgi?referer=&httpsredir=1&article=2520&context=dissertations

Monroe, V. (2024, April 29). *15 traits of an alpha female*. Everybody Loves Your Money. https://www.everybodylovesyourmoney.com/2024/04/29/15-traits-of-an-alpha-female.html

*Personality determinants of manipulative behavior in the negotiation process. State of the art.* (2018). Psychologyinrussia. https://psychologyinrussia.com/volumes/?article=1189

Pirie Jones Grossman. (2023, December 27). *Leading with heart: Heidi hicks on the power of authentic women's leadership*. Medium; Authority Magazine. https://medium.com/authority-magazine/leading-with-heart-heidi-hicks-on-the-power-of-authentic-womens-leadership-23a5fb0c65f9

Pirie Jones Grossman. (2024, March 23). *Leading with heart: Bonnie frankel on the power of authentic women's leadership*. Medium; Authority Magazine. https://medium.com/authority-magazine/leading-with-heart-bonnie-frankel-on-the-power-of-authentic-womens-leadership-d860577c40f2

Robin, M. (2022, October 31). *Aligning personal values with company core values, do no harm*. Linkedin. https://www.linkedin.com/pulse/aligning-personal-values-companys-core-do-harm-michael-robin-manning?trk=pulse-article

Robinson, L., & Smith, M. (2023, October 11). *Stress management.* HelpGuide. https://www.helpguide.org/articles/stress/stress-management.htm

Sattar, T. (2023, December 11). *Alpha female.* Medium. https://medium.com/@tarasattar.writer/alpha-female-a1f2e913f320

Segal, J., Smith, M., Robinson, L., & Boose, G. (2024, May 8). *Nonverbal communication and body language.* HelpGuide. https://www.helpguide.org/articles/relationships-communication/nonverbal-communication.htm

Segal, J., Smith, M., Robinson, L., & Shubin, J. (2024, February 5). *Improving emotional intelligence (EQ).* HelpGuide. https://www.helpguide.org/articles/mental-health/emotional-intelligence-eq.htm

Shivangisharan. (2023, August 16). *Decode the secrets of becoming a timeless femme fatale: Your ultimate guide.* Medium. https://medium.com/@shivangisharan82/decode-the-secrets-of-becoming-a-timeless-femme-fatale-your-ultimate-guide-bcadc8367cc1

Singh, S. (2024). *How can you balance assertiveness and empathy in leadership communication?* Linkedin. https://www.linkedin.com/advice/1/how-can-you-balance-assertiveness-empathy-2wwtf

Smith, M., Segal, R., Robinson, L., & Segal, J. (2019, March 13). *Building better mental health.* HelpGuide. https://www.helpguide.org/articles/mental-health/building-better-mental-health.htm

Staff. (2019, April 25). *How to influence without authority.* 3 plus International. https://3plusinternational.com/2019/04/how-to-influence-without-authority/

Sumra, M. (n.d.). *The human alpha female: Social and biological perspectives.* Retrieved January 31, 2024, from https://tspace.library.utoronto.ca/bitstream/1807/97690/1/Sumra_Monika_K_201911_PhD_thesis.pdf

Téneille Coetzer. (2024, June 2). *Emotional intelligence (EI)*. Linkedin. https://www.linkedin.com/pulse/developing-emotional-intelligence-understanding-managing-coetzer-ikevf

The Nobel Prize. (2024). *The Nobel Prize in Physics 1903*. NobelPrize.org; The Nobel Prize. https://www.nobelprize.org/prizes/physics/1903/marie-curie/biographical/

Vader, K. (2019, August 12). *Emotional intelligence in love and relationships*. Helpguide. https://www.helpguide.org/articles/mental-health/emotional-intelligence-love-relationships.htm

Van Edwards, V. (2012, February 8). *The alpha female: 9 ways you can tell who is an alpha woman*. Science of People. https://www.scienceofpeople.com/alpha-female/

WE Staff. (2024). *Women entrepreneurs review*. Women Entrepreneurs Review. https://www.womenentrepreneursreview.com/viewpoint/experts-column/emotional-intelligence-empowering-women-s-success-in-business-leadership-nwid-3674.html

Wikipedia. (2021, October 17). *Manipulation (psychology)*. Wikipedia. https://en.wikipedia.org/wiki/Manipulation_(psychology)

Wikipedia Contributors. (2019, March 19). *Social influence*. Wikipedia; Wikimedia Foundation. https://en.wikipedia.org/wiki/Social_influence

Wikipedia Contributors. (2024, January 28). *Emotional blackmail*. Wikipedia; Wikimedia Foundation. https://en.wikipedia.org/wiki/Emotional_blackmail

Wikipedia Contributors. (n.d.-a). *Sheryl Sandberg*. Wikipedia; Wikimedia Foundation. https://en.wikipedia.org/wiki/Sheryl_Sandberg

Wikipedia Contributors. (n.d.-b). *Malala Yousafzai*. Wikipedia; Wikimedia Foundation. https://en.wikipedia.org/wiki/Malala_Yousafzai

Women of Influence. (2024, April 23). *Personal branding in the digital age: Five strategic approaches to...* Women of Influence. https://www.womenofinfluence.ca/2024/04/23/personal-branding-in-the-digital-age-five-strategic-approaches-to-elevate-your-online-presence-and-influence/